thich nhat hanh's
little book of
selected quotes

For things to reveal themselves to us, we need to be ready to abandon our views about them.

thich nhat hanh's little book of selected quotes

To be beautiful means to be yourself. You don't need to be accepted by others. You need to accept yourself.

thich nhat hanh's little book of selected quotes

Life can be found only in the present moment. The past is gone, the future is not yet here, and if we do not go back to ourselves in the present moment, we cannot be in touch with life.

thich nhat hanh's little book of selected quotes

The seven factors of Awakening are mindfulness, investigation of phenomena, diligence, joy, ease, concentration, and letting go.

thich nhat hanh's little book of selected quotes

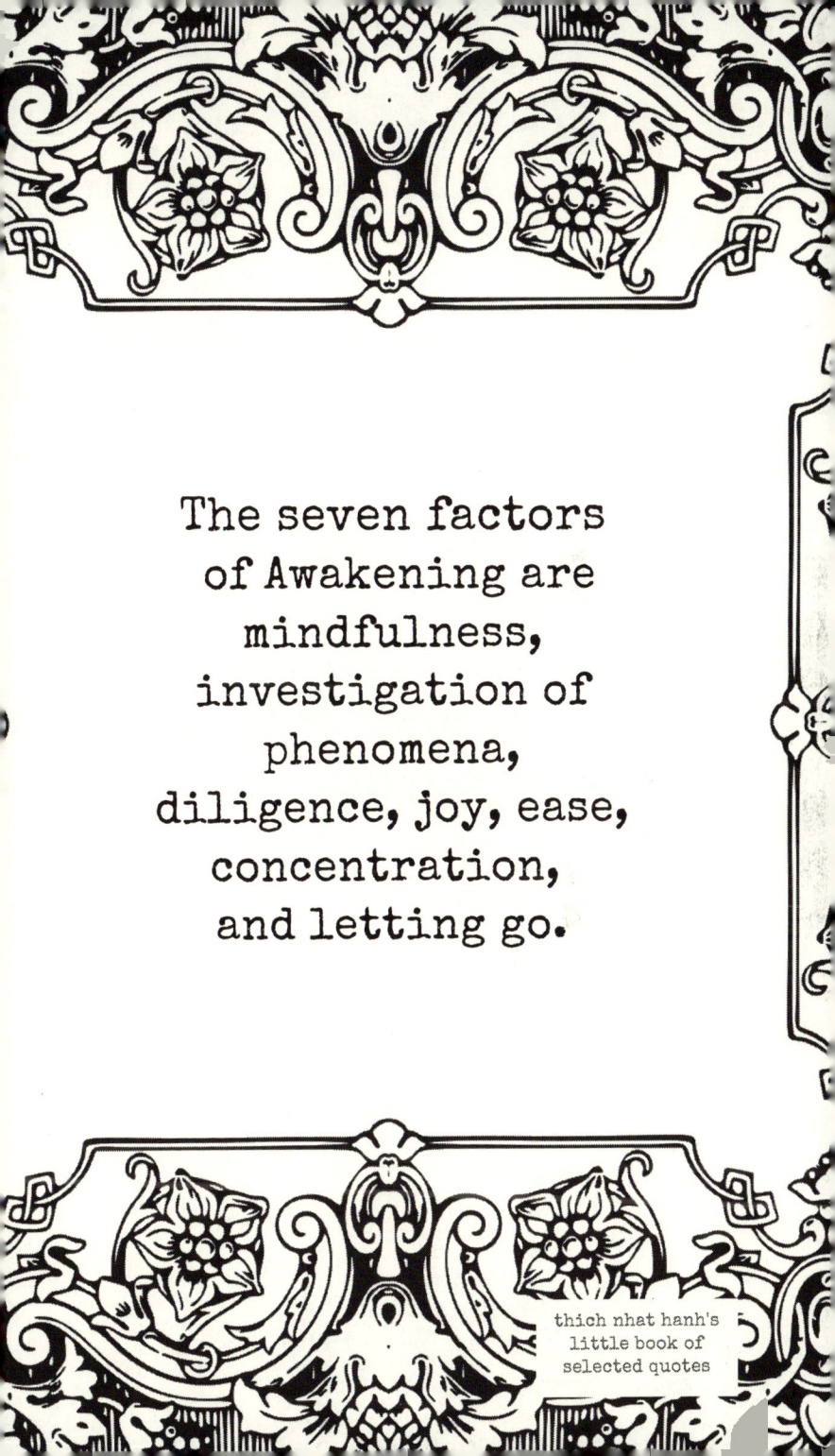

In true love,
you attain
freedom.

thich nhat hanh's
little book of
selected quotes

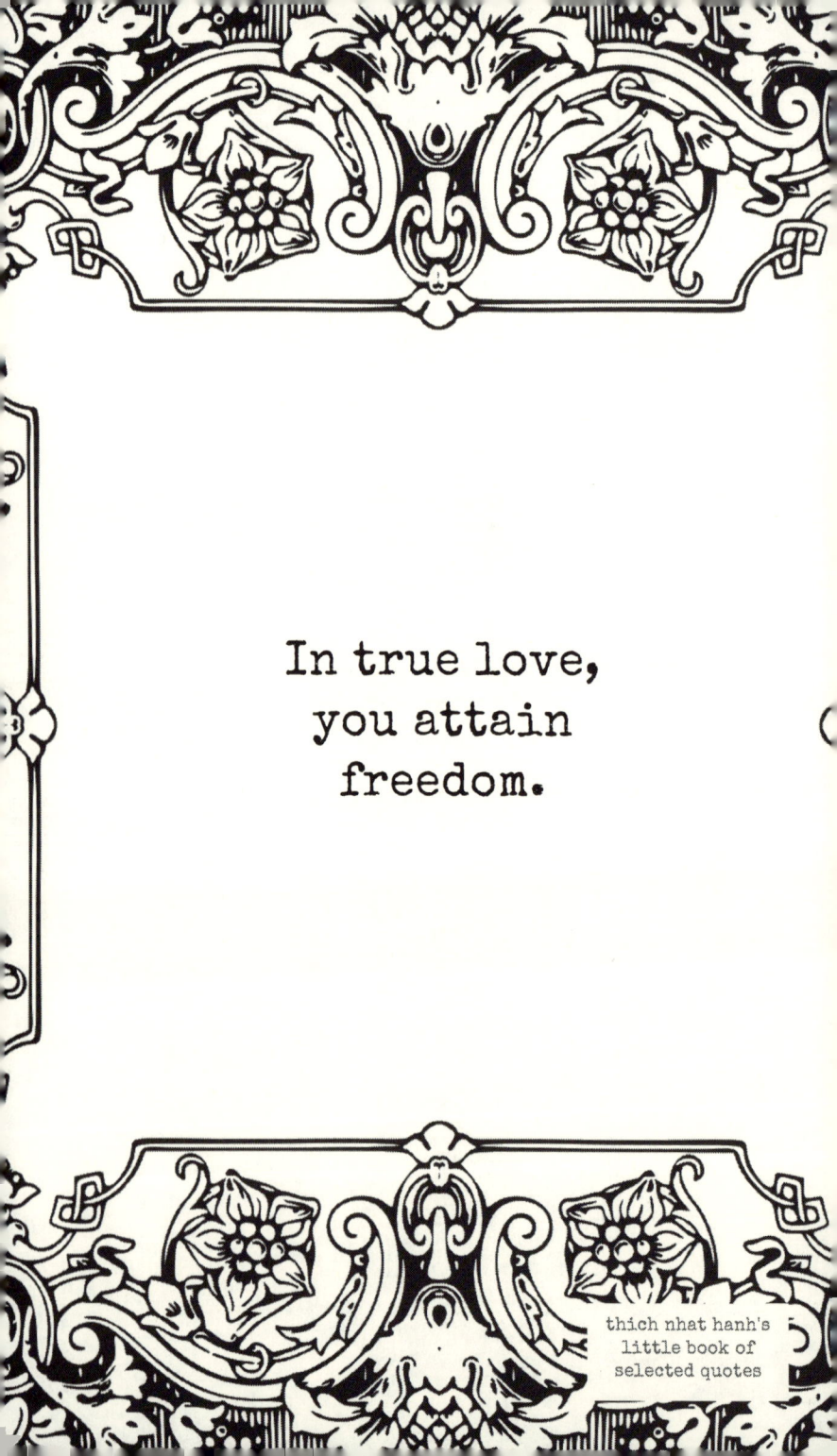

The true miracle is
not walking on water
or walking in air,
but simply walking
on this earth.

thich nhat hanh's
little book of
selected quotes

Peace is present right here and now, in ourselves and in everything we do and see. Every breath we take, every step we take, can be filled with peace, joy, and serenity. The question is whether or not we are in touch with it. We need only to be awake, alive in the present moment.

thich nhat hanh's little book of selected quotes

Root out the violence in your life, and learn to live compassionately and mindfully. Seek peace. When you have peace within, real peace with others is possible.

thich nhat hanh's little book of selected quotes

Being rich is an obstacle to loving. When you are rich, you want to continue to be rich, and so you end up devoting all your time, all your energy, in your daily life to stay rich.

thich nhat hanh's little book of selected quotes

When our beliefs are based on our own direct experience of reality and not on notions offered by others, no one can remove these beliefs from us.

thich nhat hanh's little book of selected quotes

When another person makes you suffer, it is because he suffers deeply within himself, and his suffering is spilling over. He does not need punishment; he needs help. That's the message he is sending.

thich nhat hanh's little book of selected quotes

Take my hand. We will walk. We will only walk. We will enjoy our walk without thinking of arriving anywhere.

thich nhat hanh's little book of selected quotes

While you are walking,
smile and be in the here
and now, and you will
transform that place
into paradise.

thich nhat hanh's
little book of
selected quotes

Thanks to impermanence, everything is possible.

thich nhat hanh's little book of selected quotes

Mindfulness is like that—it is the miracle which can call back in a flash our dispersed mind and restore it to wholeness so that we can live each minute of life.

thich nhat hanh's little book of selected quotes

People suffer because they are caught in their views. As soon as we release those views, we are free and we don't suffer anymore.

thich nhat hanh's little book of selected quotes

Birth is okay and death is okay, if we know that they are only concepts in our mind. Reality transcends both birth and death.

thich nhat hanh's little book of selected quotes

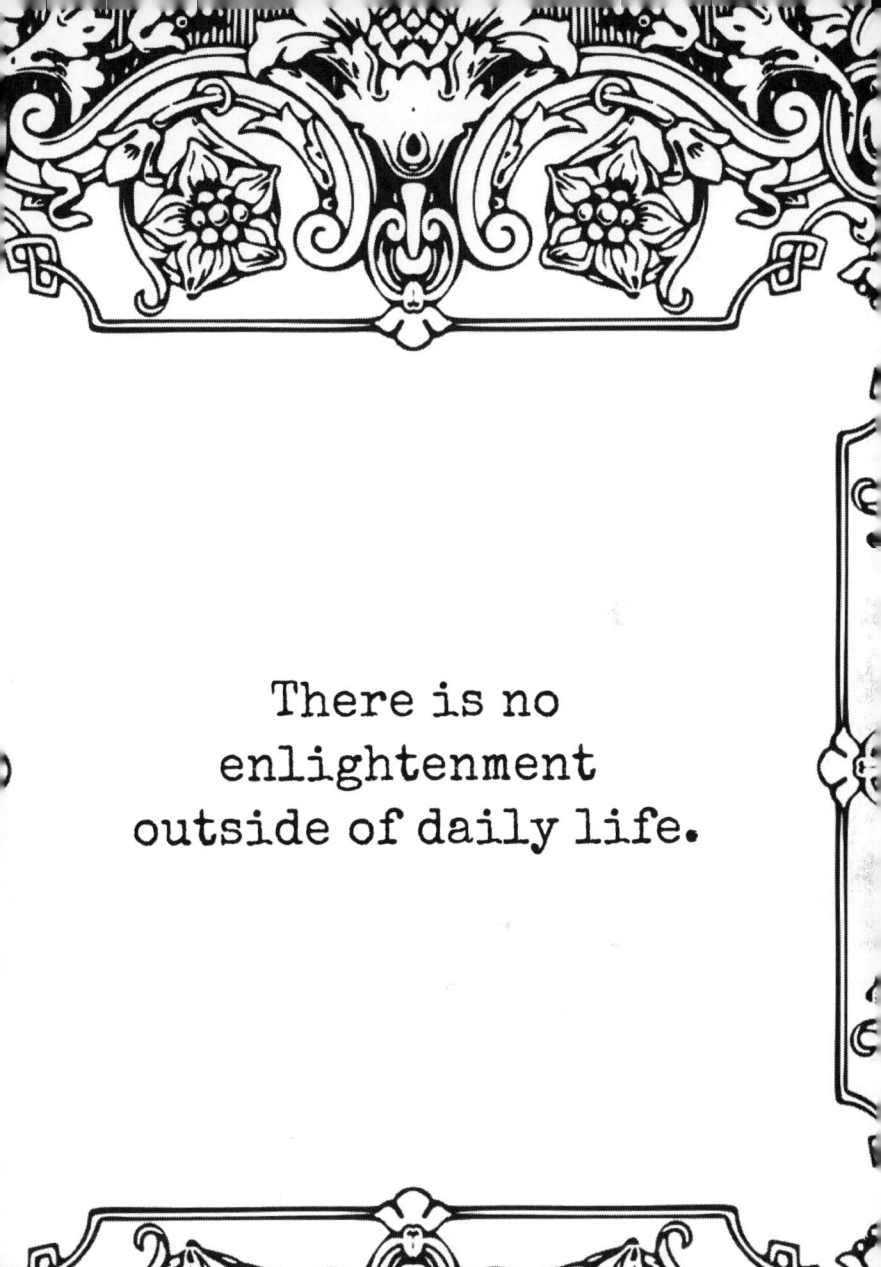

There is no
enlightenment
outside of daily life.

thich nhat hanh's
little book of
selected quotes

Often we tell ourselves, don't just sit there, do something! But when we practice awareness, we discover that the opposite may be more helpful: Don't just do something, sit there!

thich nhat hanh's little book of selected quotes

Your breathing should flow gracefully, like a river, like a water snake crossing the water, and not like a chain of rugged mountains or the gallop of a horse. To master our breath is to be in control of our bodies and minds.

thich nhat hanh's little book of selected quotes

Anger is like a storm rising up from the bottom of your consciousness. When you feel it coming, turn your focus to your breath.

thich nhat hanh's little book of selected quotes

It is said that God has created man in his own image. But it may be that humankind has created God in the image of humankind.

thich nhat hanh's little book of selected quotes

Until there is peace
between religions,
there can be no peace
in the world.

thich nhat hanh's
little book of
selected quotes

Hope is important because it can make the present moment less difficult to bear. If we believe that tomorrow will be better, we can bear a hardship today.

thich nhat hanh's little book of selected quotes

Through my love for you,
I want to express my love for
the whole cosmos, the whole
of humanity, and all beings.
By living with you, I want to
learn to love everyone and
all species. If I succeed in
loving you, I will be able to
love everyone and all
species on Earth... This is
the real message of love.

thich nhat hanh's
little book of
selected quotes

We have to learn to live our life as a human being deeply. We need to live each breath deeply so that we have peace, joy and freedom as we breathe.

thich nhat hanh's little book of selected quotes

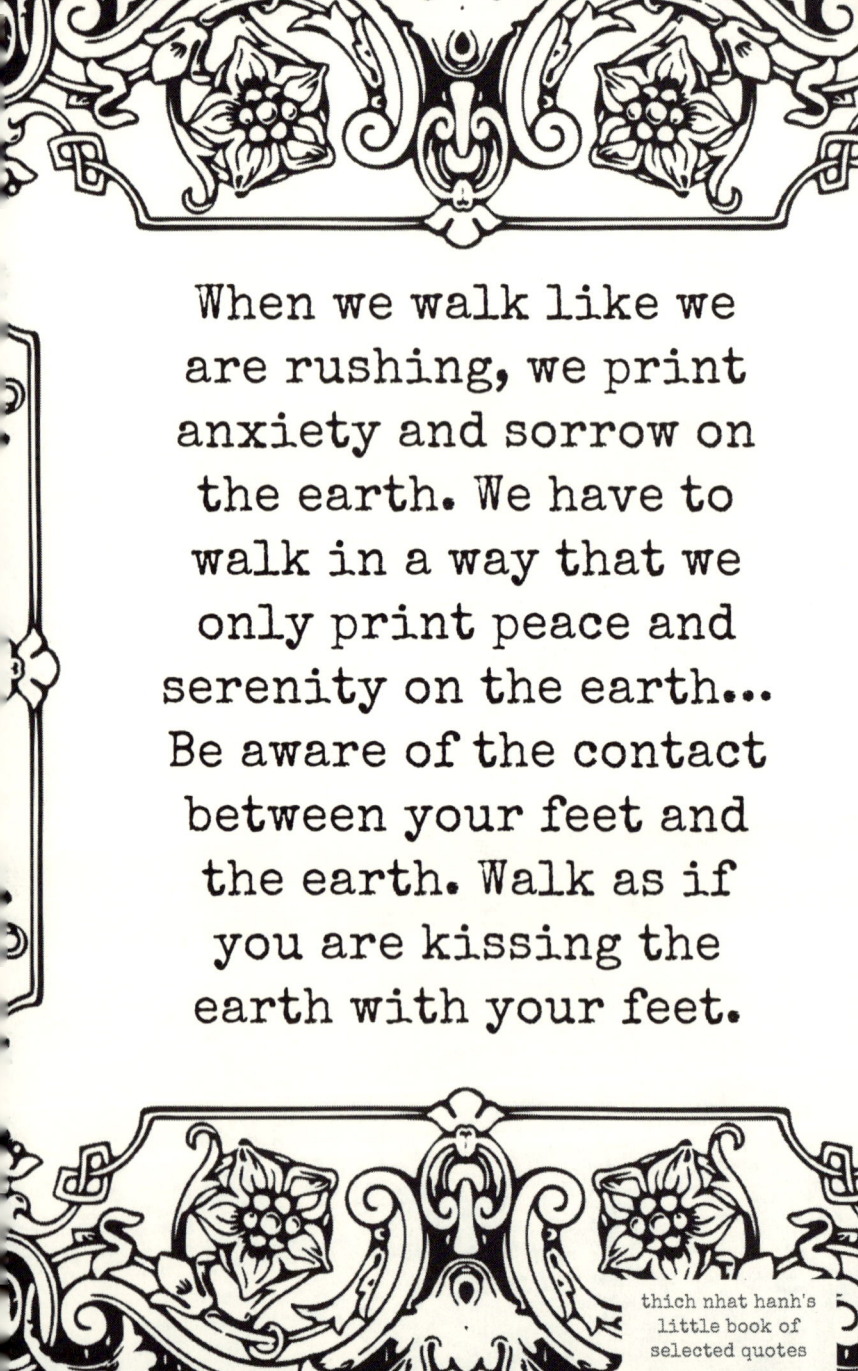

When we walk like we are rushing, we print anxiety and sorrow on the earth. We have to walk in a way that we only print peace and serenity on the earth... Be aware of the contact between your feet and the earth. Walk as if you are kissing the earth with your feet.

thich nhat hanh's little book of selected quotes

Keeping your body healthy is an expression of gratitude to the whole cosmos — the trees, the clouds, everything.

thich nhat hanh's little book of selected quotes

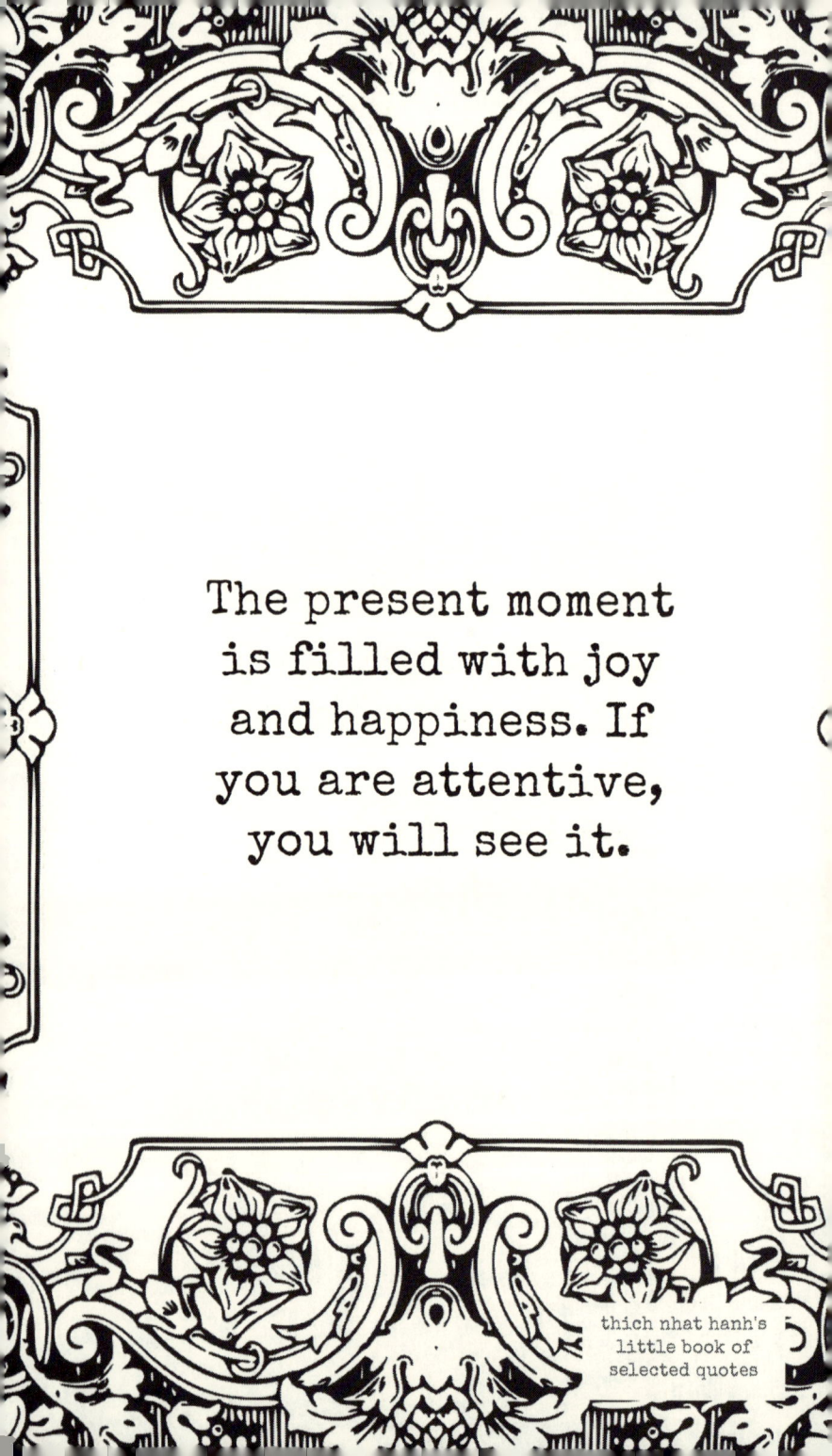

The present moment is filled with joy and happiness. If you are attentive, you will see it.

thich nhat hanh's little book of selected quotes

Walk as if you are
kissing the Earth
with your feet.

thich nhat hanh's
little book of
selected quotes

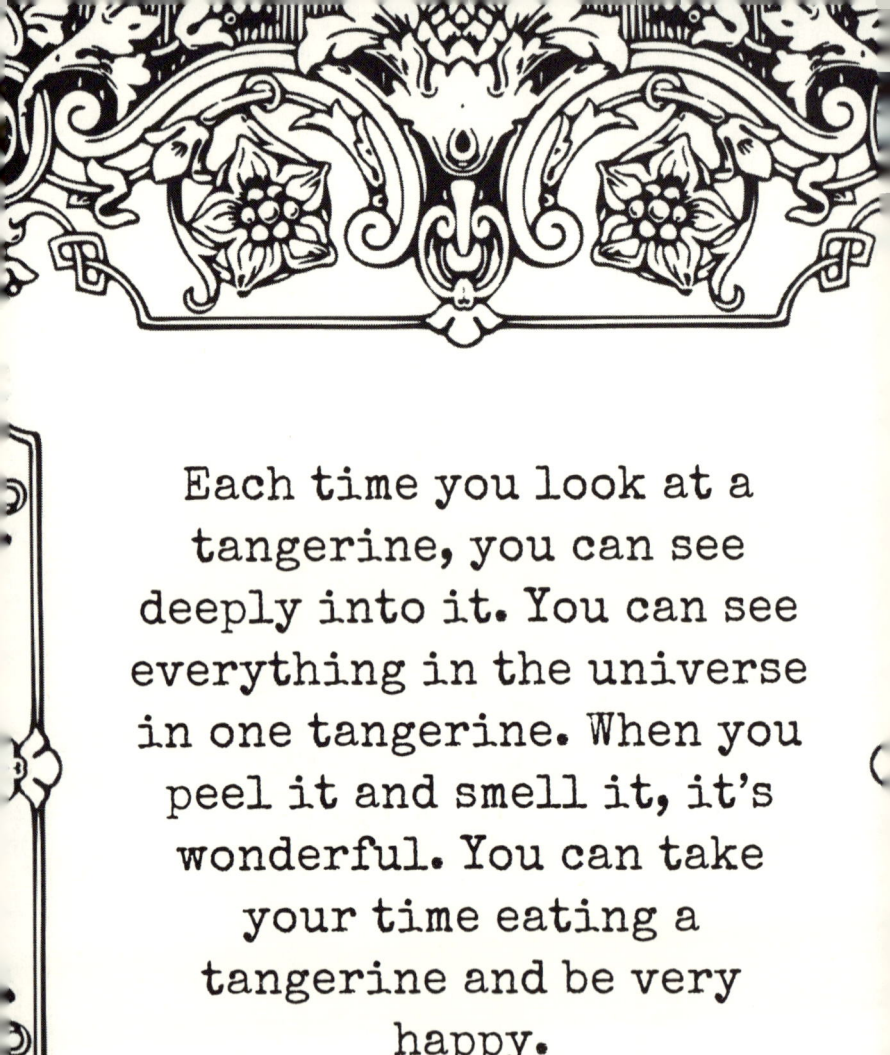

Each time you look at a tangerine, you can see deeply into it. You can see everything in the universe in one tangerine. When you peel it and smell it, it's wonderful. You can take your time eating a tangerine and be very happy.

thich nhat hanh's little book of selected quotes

You must love in such a way that the person you love feels free.

thich nhat hanh's little book of selected quotes

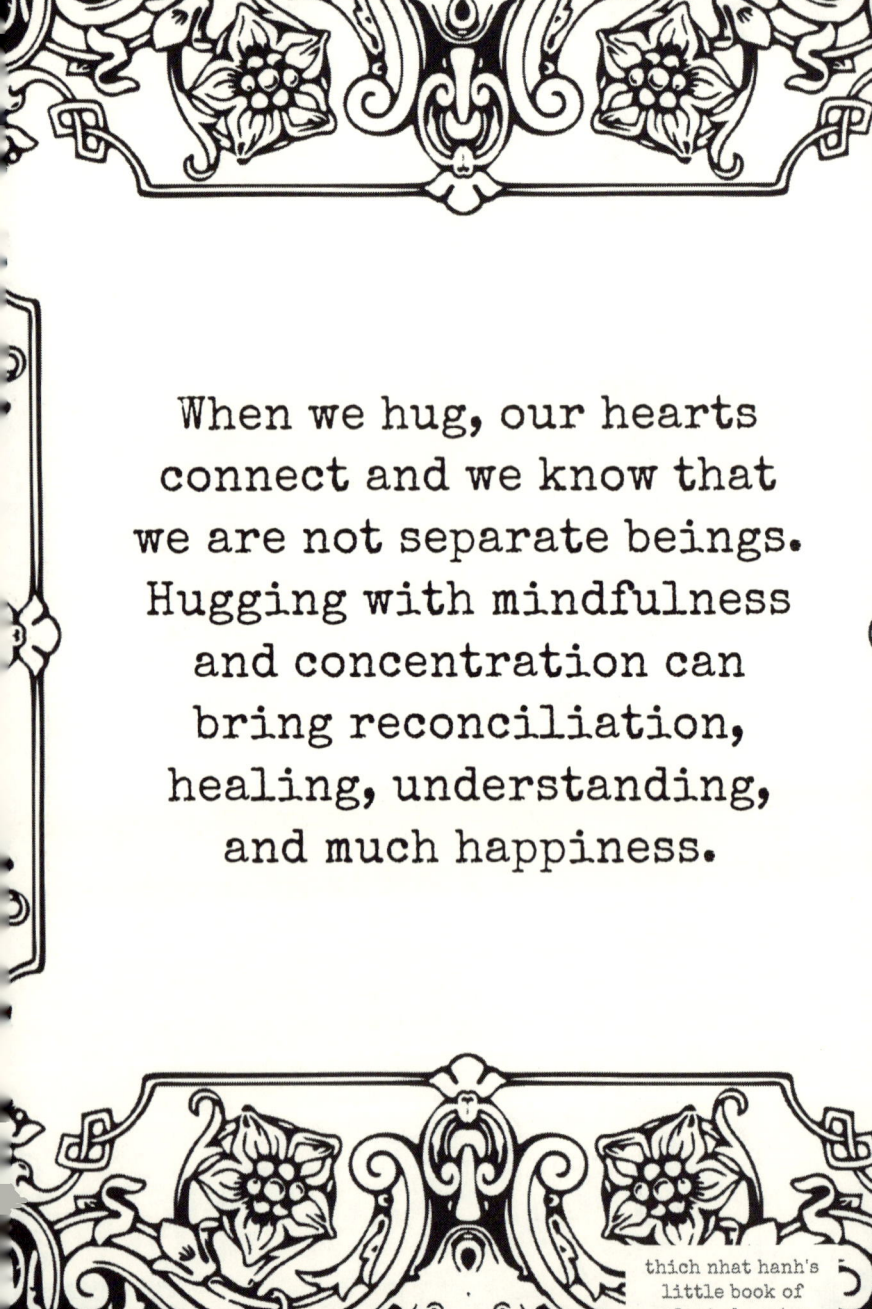

When we hug, our hearts connect and we know that we are not separate beings. Hugging with mindfulness and concentration can bring reconciliation, healing, understanding, and much happiness.

thich nhat hanh's little book of selected quotes

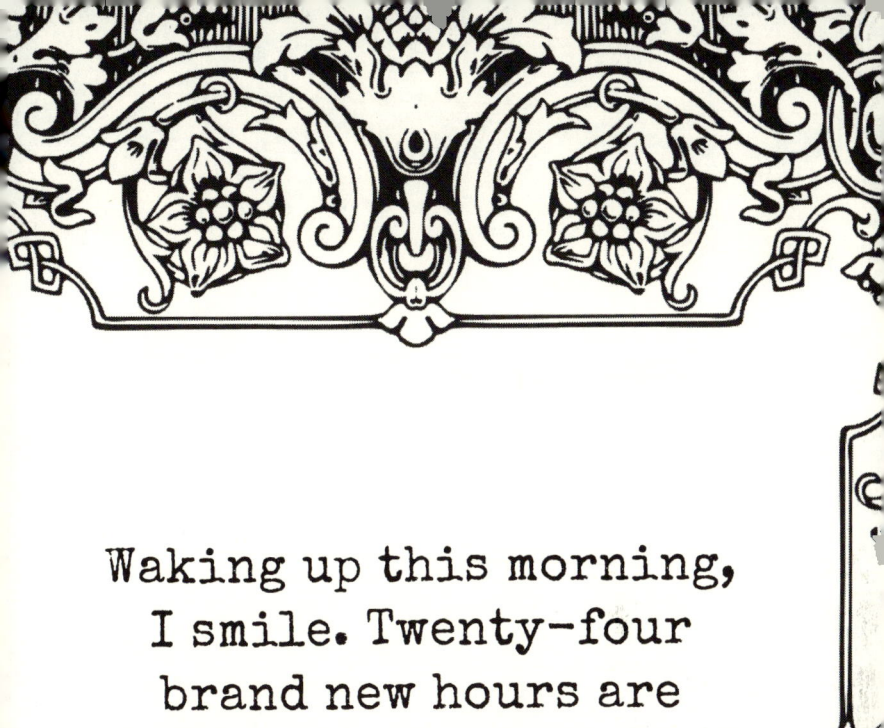

Waking up this morning, I smile. Twenty-four brand new hours are before me. I vow to live fully in each moment and to look at all beings with eyes of compassion.

thich nhat hanh's little book of selected quotes

Drink your tea slowly and reverently, as if it is the axis on which the whole earth revolves – slowly, evenly, without rushing toward the future.

thich nhat hanh's little book of selected quotes

You are me, and I am you.
Isn't it obvious that we
"inter-are"?
You cultivate the flower
in yourself, so that
I will be beautiful.
I transform the garbage
in myself, so that you
will not have to suffer.

thich nhat hanh's
little book of
selected quotes

Smile, breathe,
and go slowly.

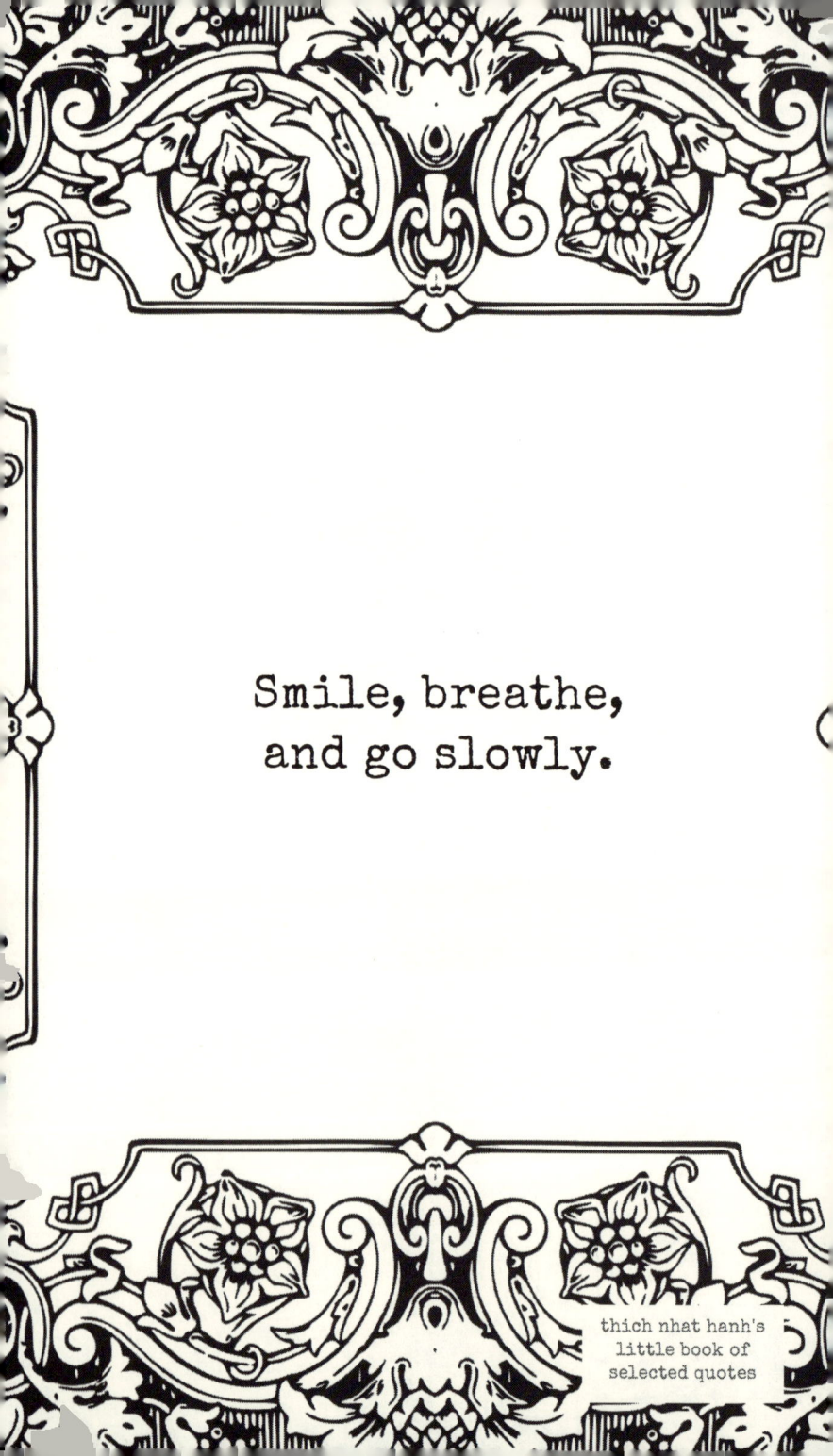

thich nhat hanh's
little book of
selected quotes

Breathing in, I calm body and mind. Breathing out, I smile. Dwelling in the present moment I know this is the only moment.

thich nhat hanh's little book of selected quotes

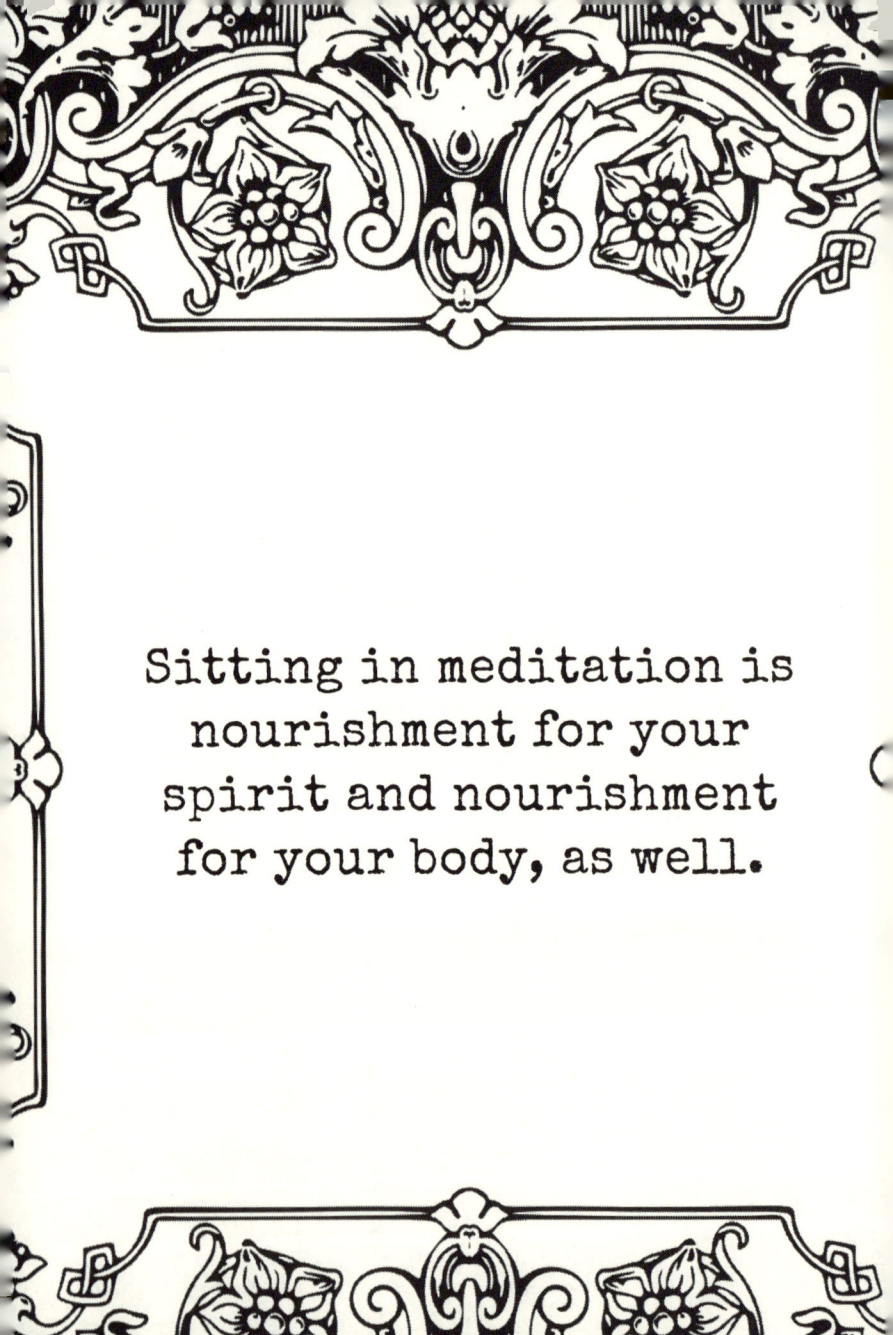

Sitting in meditation is nourishment for your spirit and nourishment for your body, as well.

thich nhat hanh's little book of selected quotes

The source of love is deep in us and we can help others realize a lot of happiness. One word, one action, one thought can reduce another person's suffering and bring that person joy.

thich nhat hanh's little book of selected quotes

True love always brings joy to ourselves and to the one we love. If our love does not bring joy to both of us, it is not true love.

thich nhat hanh's little book of selected quotes

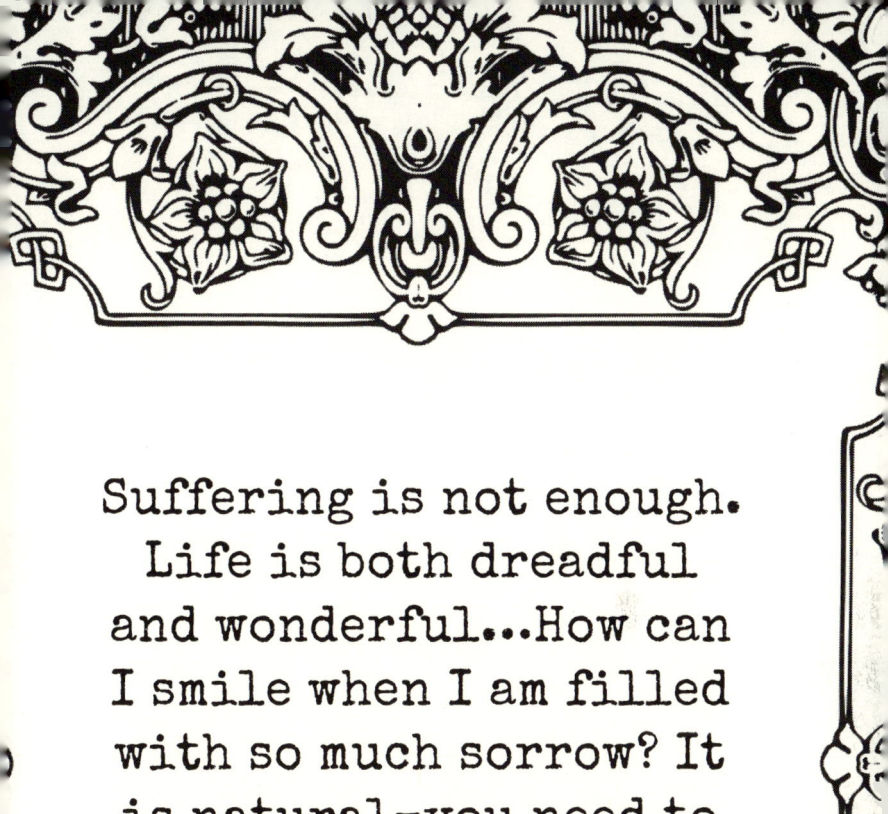

Suffering is not enough. Life is both dreadful and wonderful...How can I smile when I am filled with so much sorrow? It is natural—you need to smile to your sorrow because you are more than your sorrow.

thich nhat hanh's little book of selected quotes

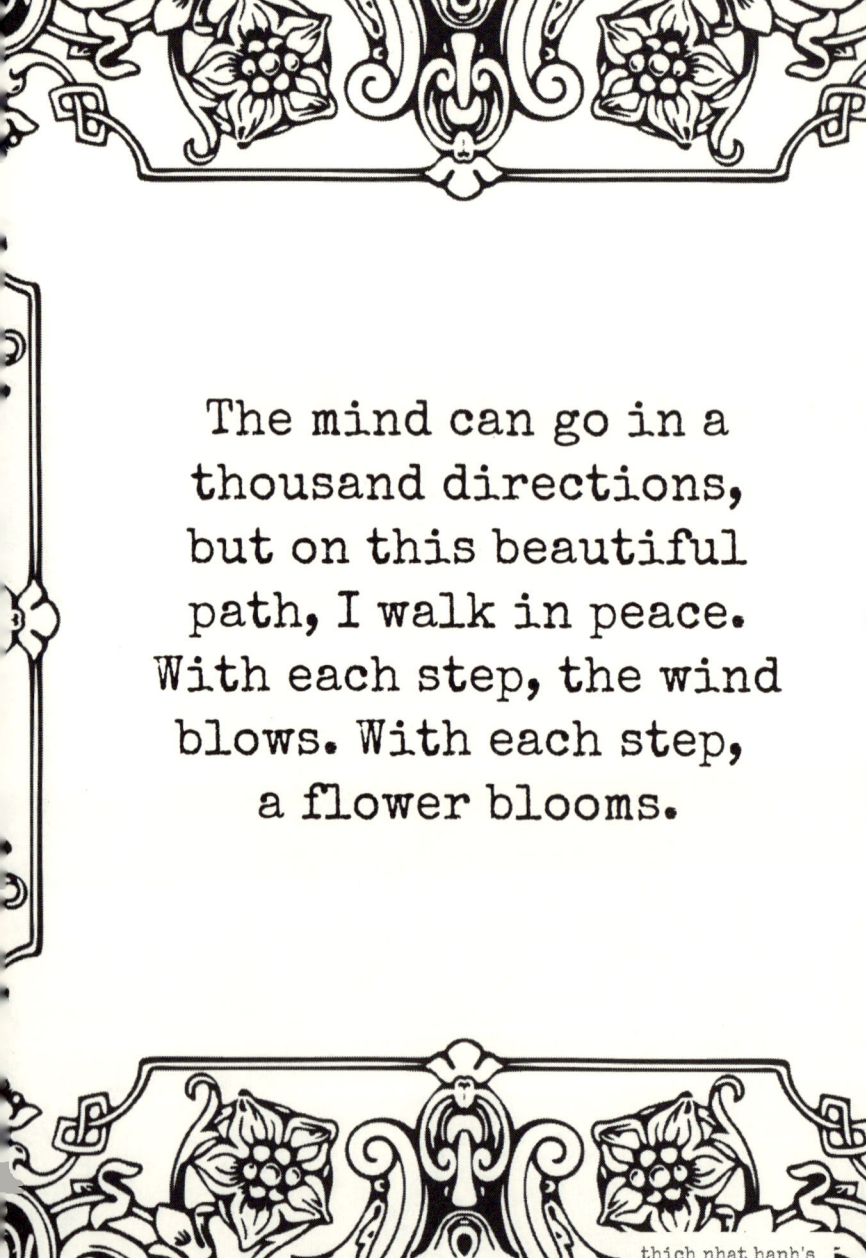

The mind can go in a thousand directions, but on this beautiful path, I walk in peace. With each step, the wind blows. With each step, a flower blooms.

thich nhat hanh's little book of selected quotes

If our love is only a will to possess, it is not love.

thich nhat hanh's little book of selected quotes

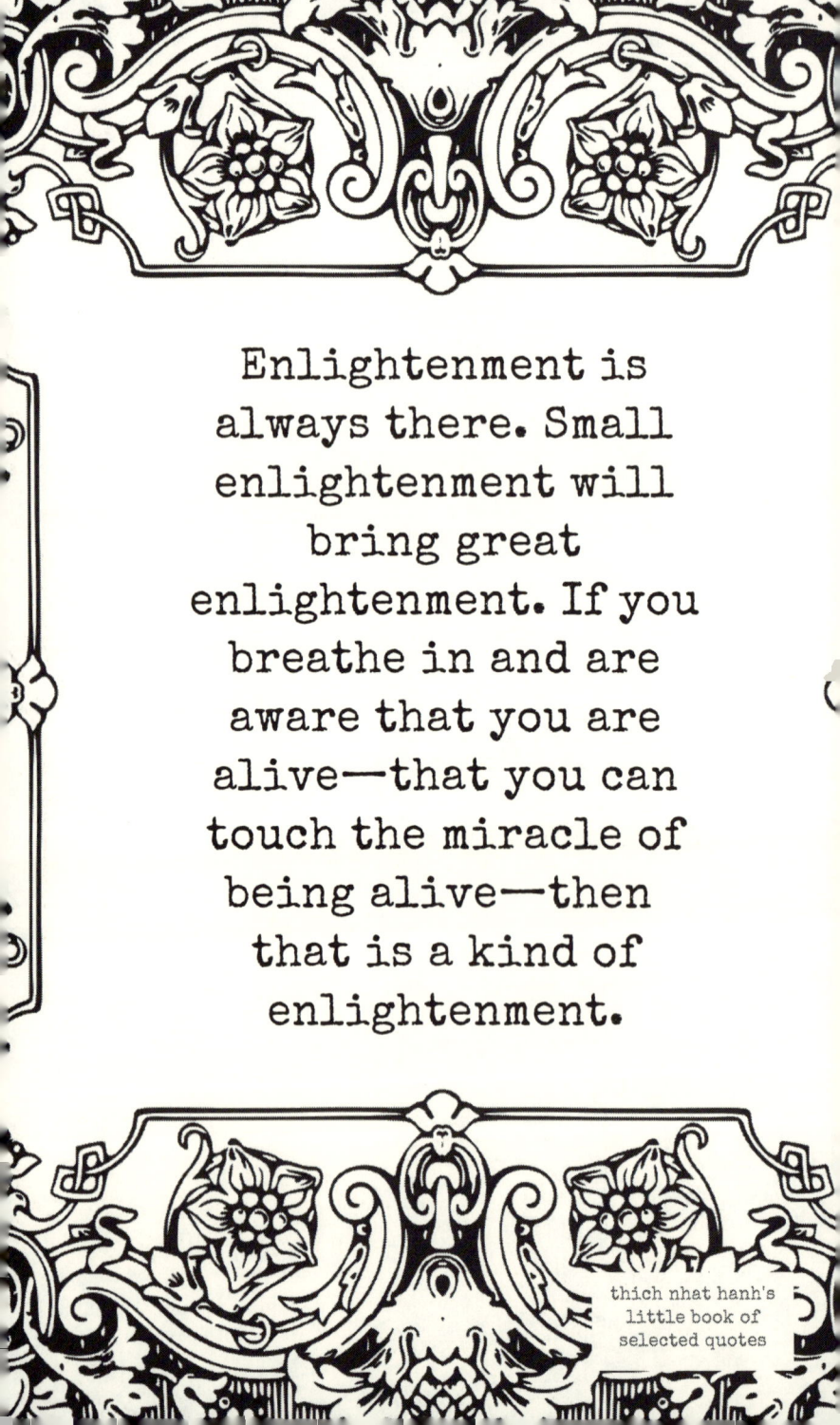

Enlightenment is always there. Small enlightenment will bring great enlightenment. If you breathe in and are aware that you are alive—that you can touch the miracle of being alive—then that is a kind of enlightenment.

thich nhat hanh's little book of selected quotes

The secret of Buddhism is to remove all ideas, all concepts, in order for the truth to have a chance to penetrate, to reveal itself.

thich nhat hanh's little book of selected quotes

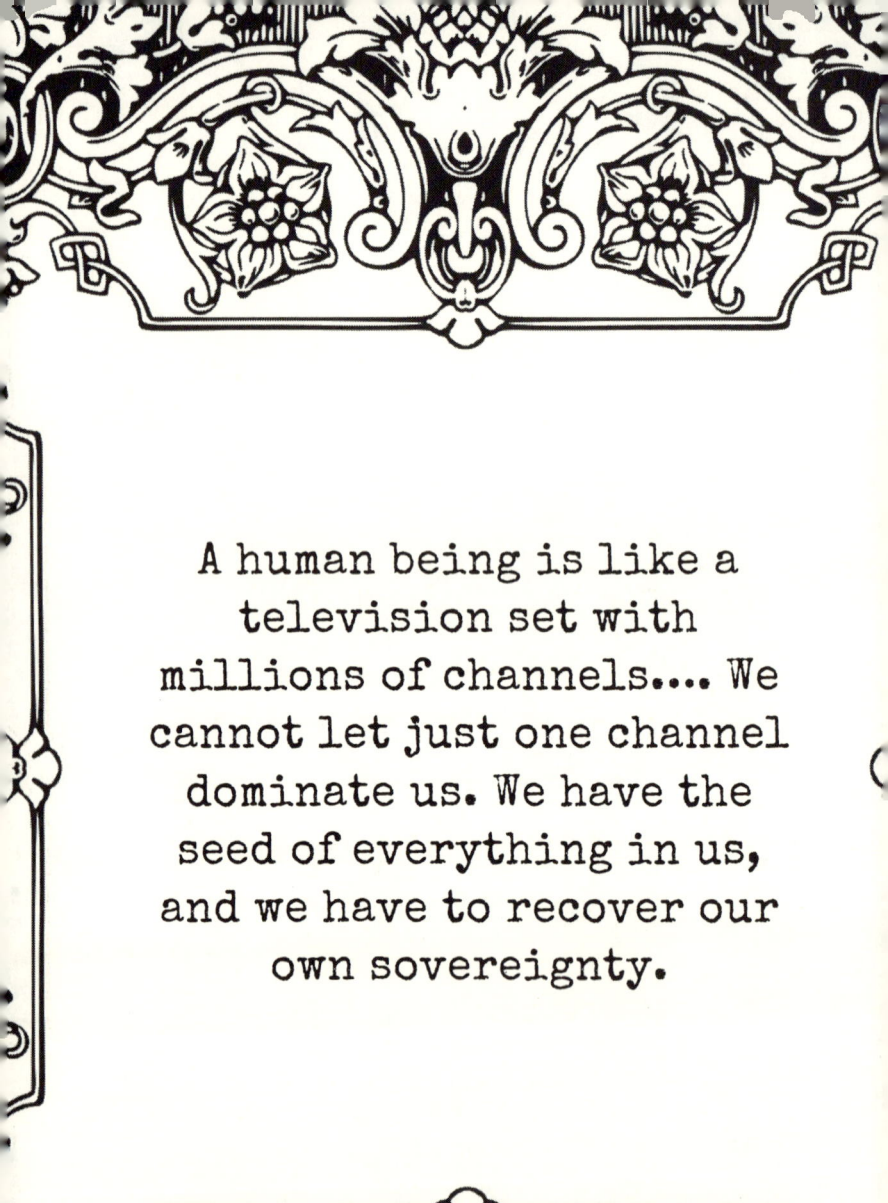

A human being is like a television set with millions of channels.... We cannot let just one channel dominate us. We have the seed of everything in us, and we have to recover our own sovereignty.

thich nhat hanh's little book of selected quotes

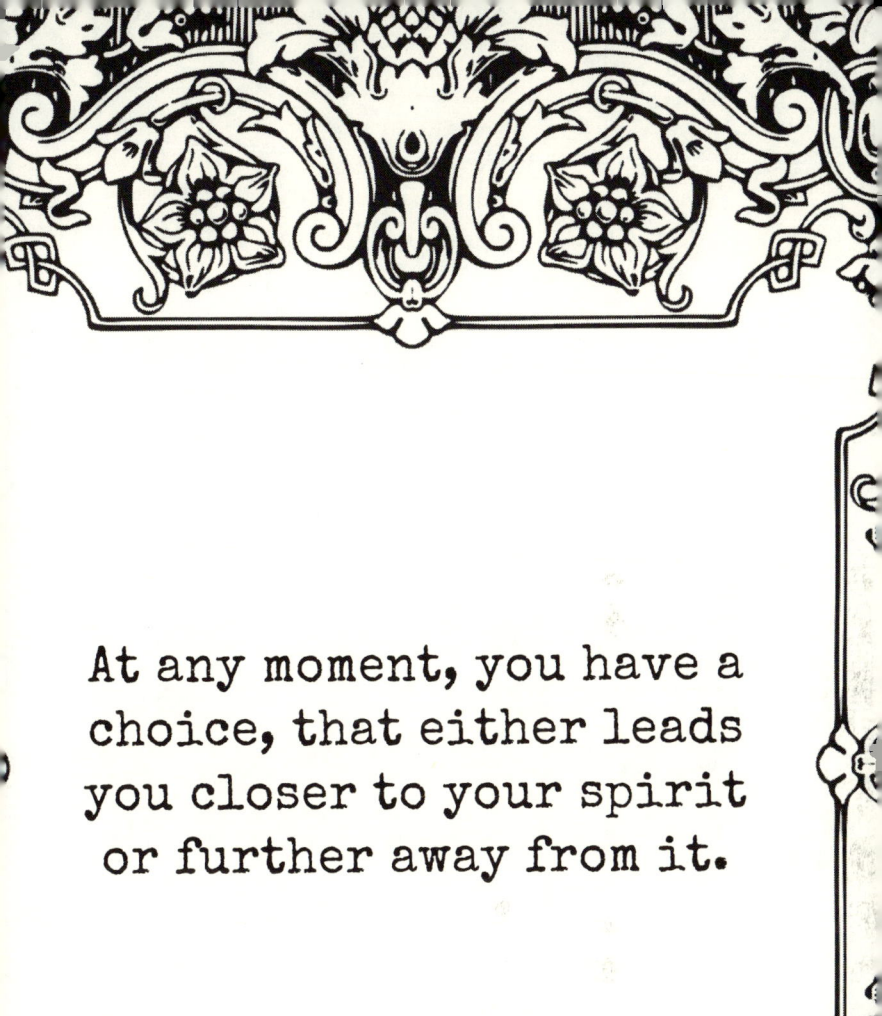

At any moment, you have a choice, that either leads you closer to your spirit or further away from it.

thich nhat hanh's
little book of
selected quotes

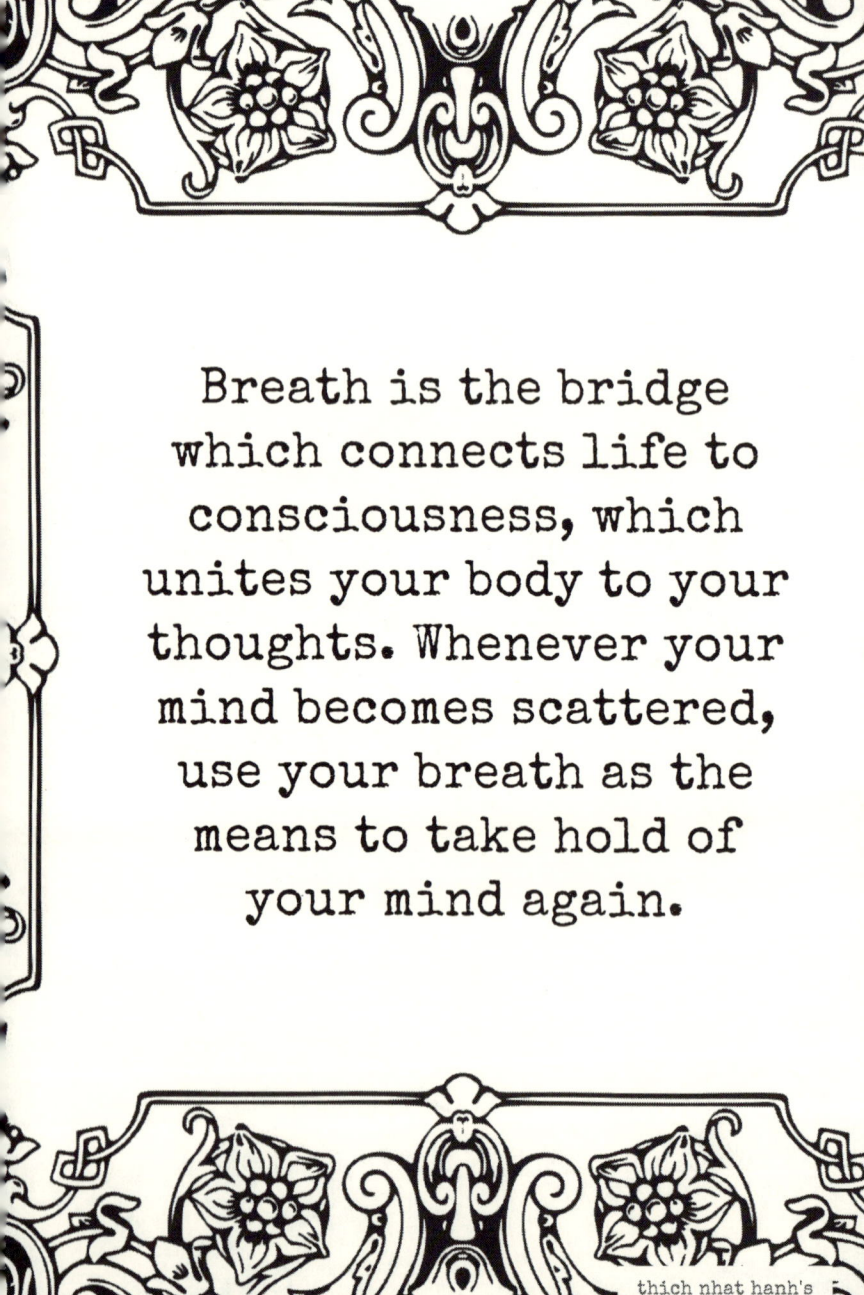

Breath is the bridge which connects life to consciousness, which unites your body to your thoughts. Whenever your mind becomes scattered, use your breath as the means to take hold of your mind again.

thich nhat hanh's little book of selected quotes

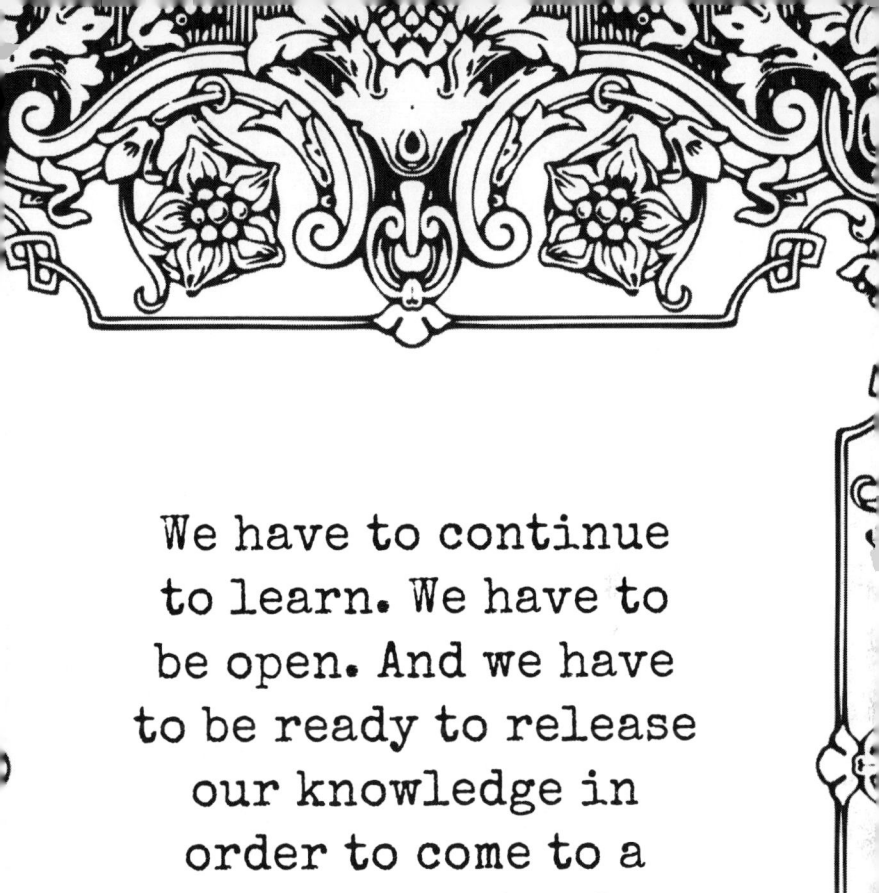

We have to continue to learn. We have to be open. And we have to be ready to release our knowledge in order to come to a higher understanding of reality.

thich nhat hanh's little book of selected quotes

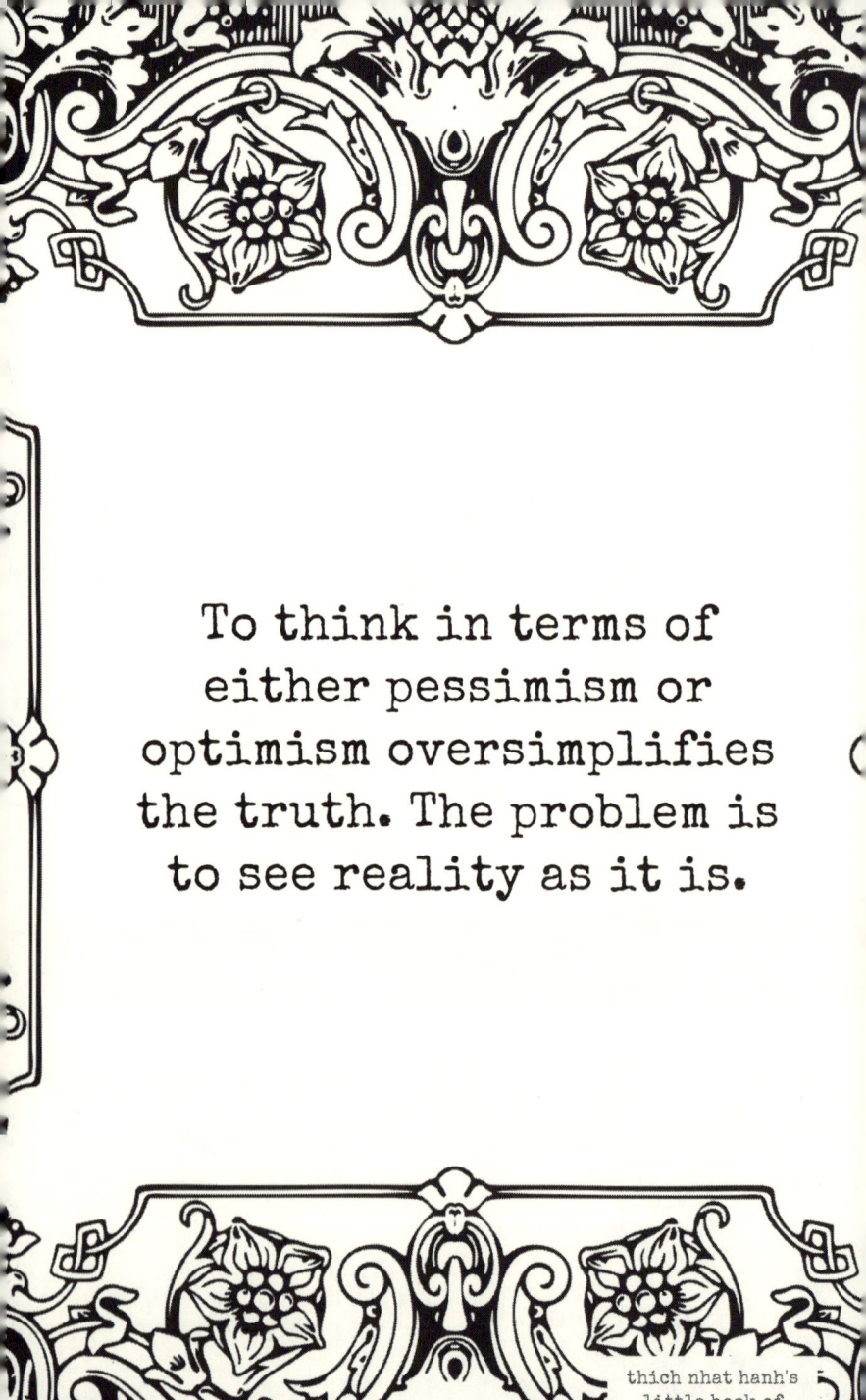

To think in terms of either pessimism or optimism oversimplifies the truth. The problem is to see reality as it is.

thich nhat hanh's little book of selected quotes

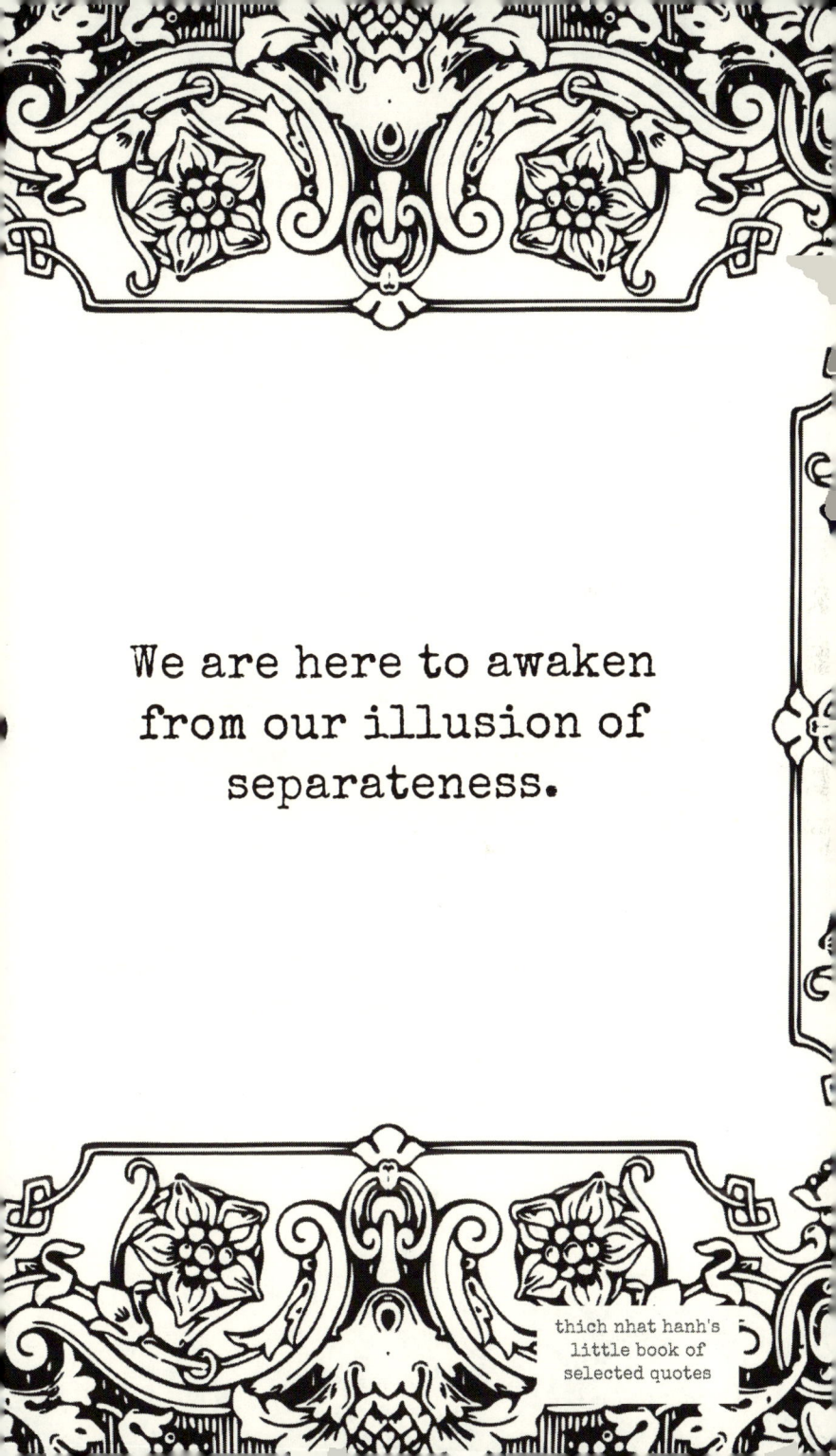

We are here to awaken from our illusion of separateness.

thich nhat hanh's
little book of
selected quotes

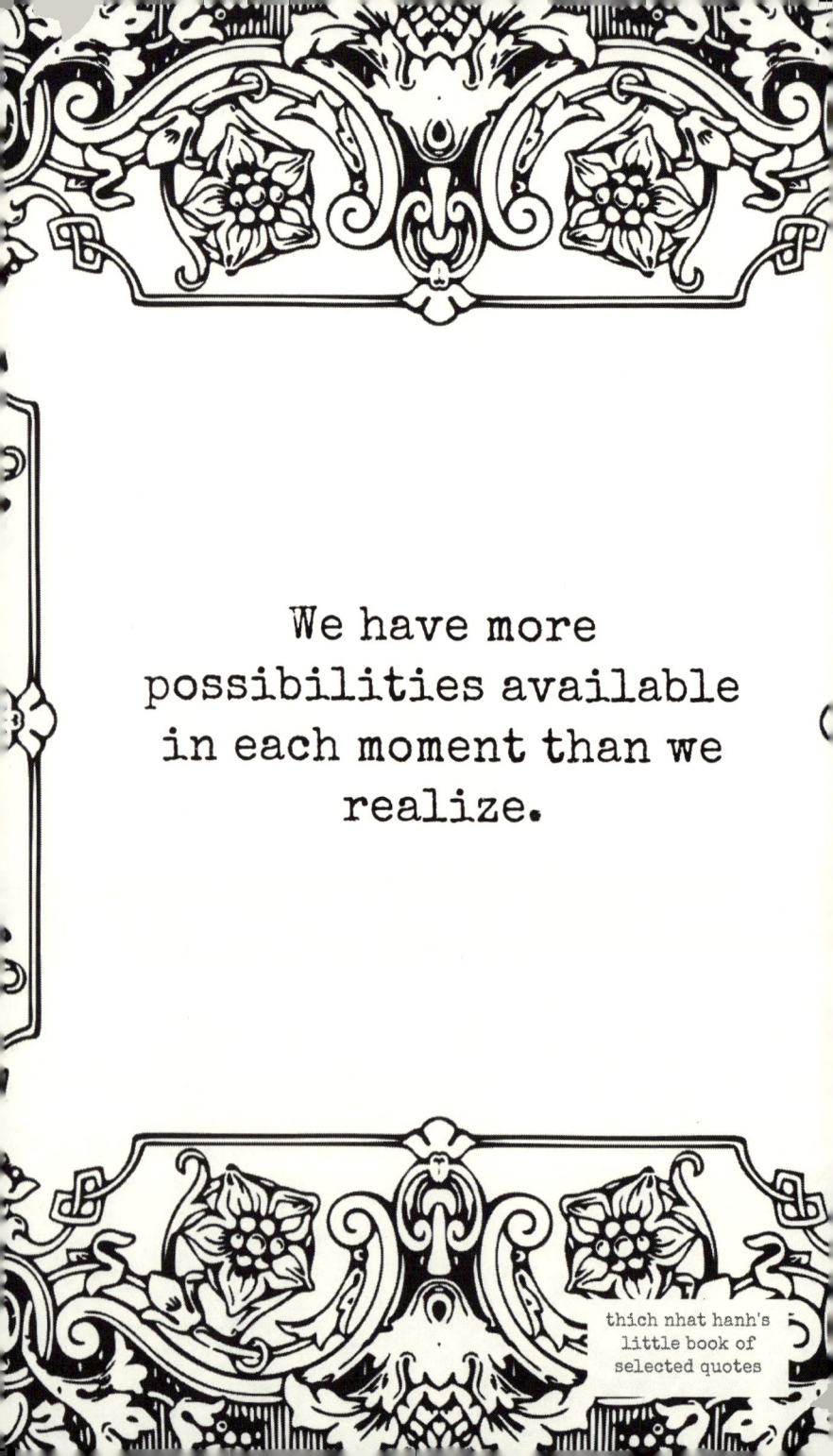

We have more possibilities available in each moment than we realize.

thich nhat hanh's little book of selected quotes

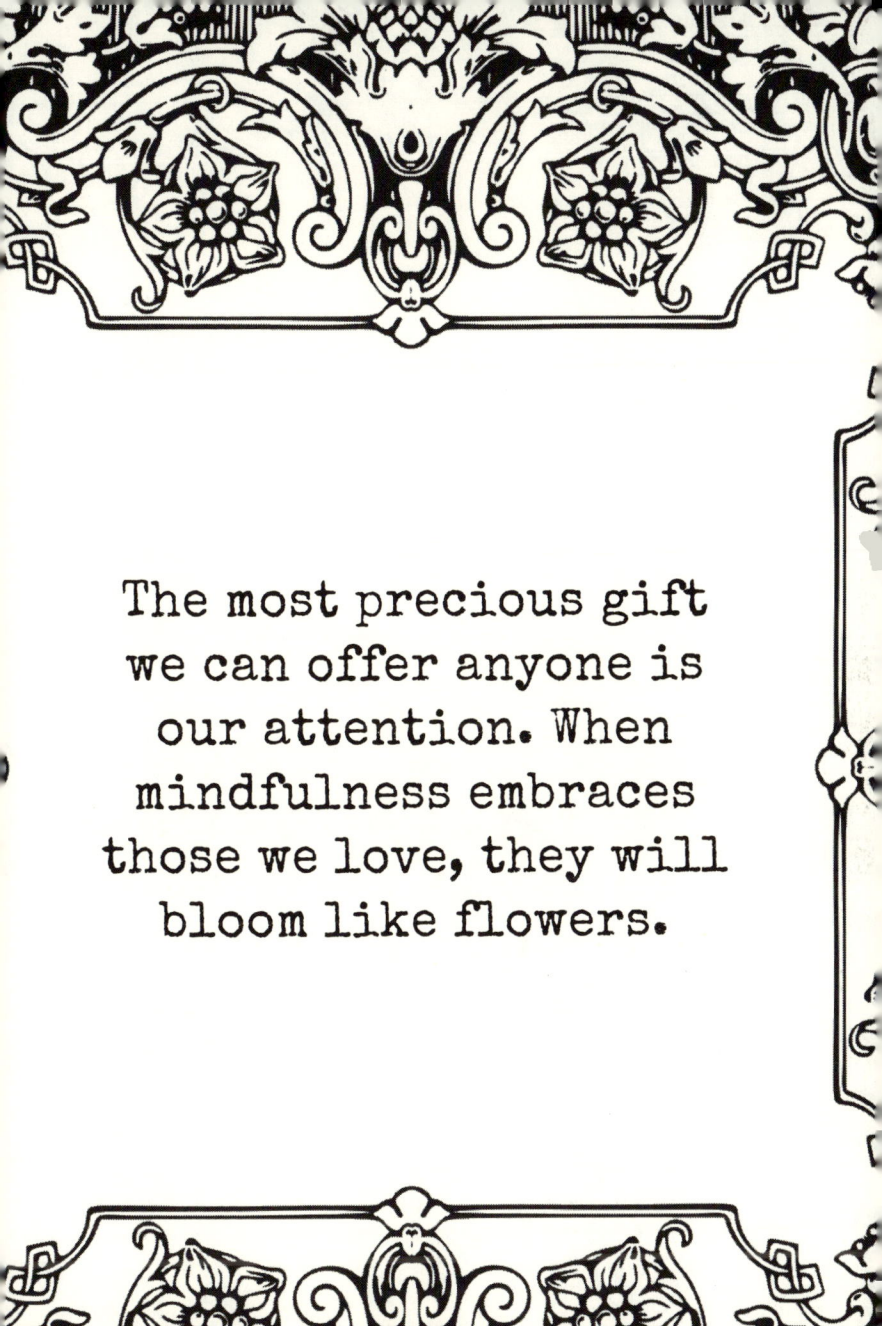

The most precious gift we can offer anyone is our attention. When mindfulness embraces those we love, they will bloom like flowers.

thich nhat hanh's little book of selected quotes

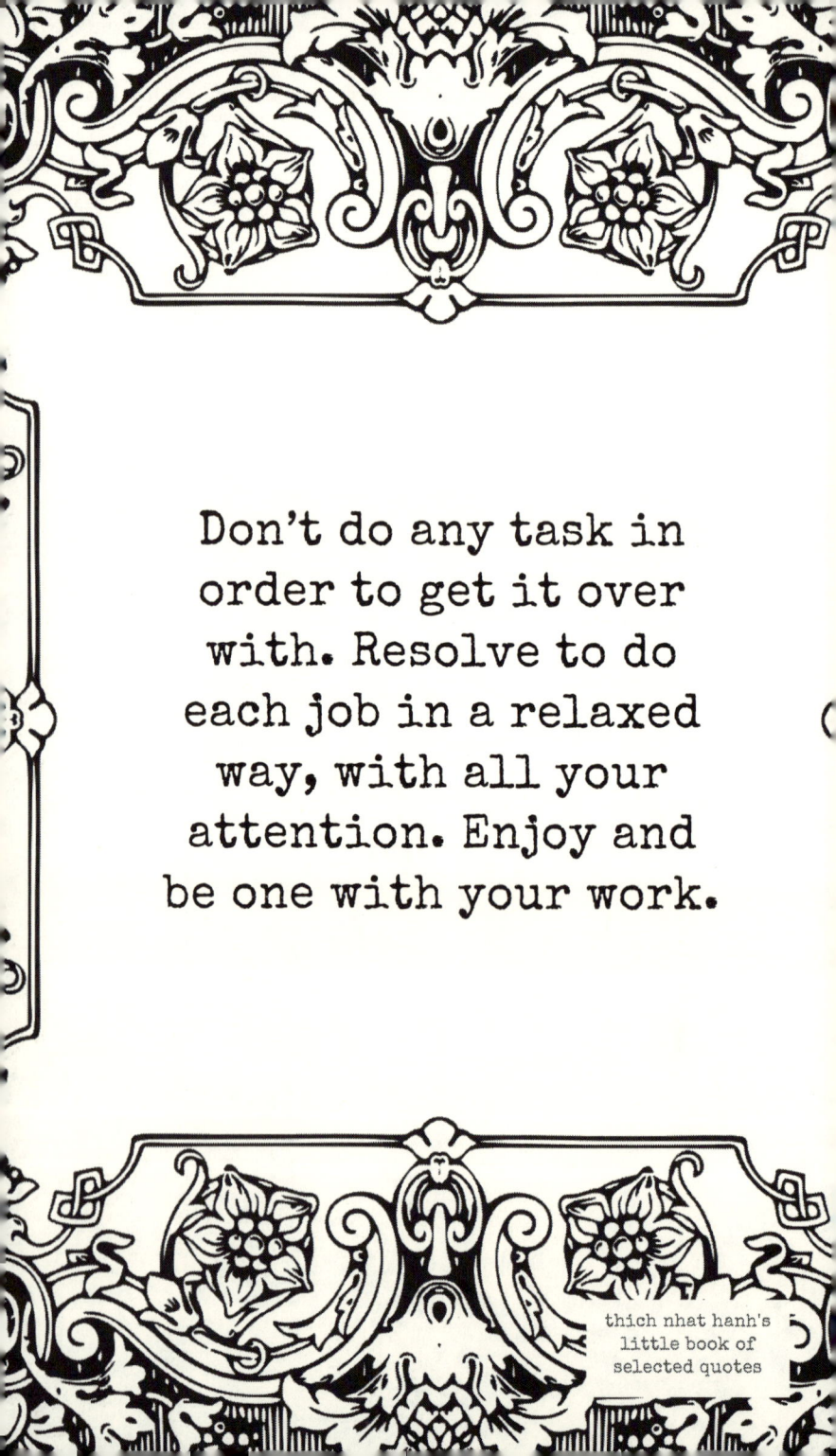

Don't do any task in order to get it over with. Resolve to do each job in a relaxed way, with all your attention. Enjoy and be one with your work.

thich nhat hanh's little book of selected quotes

Life is available only in the present moment.

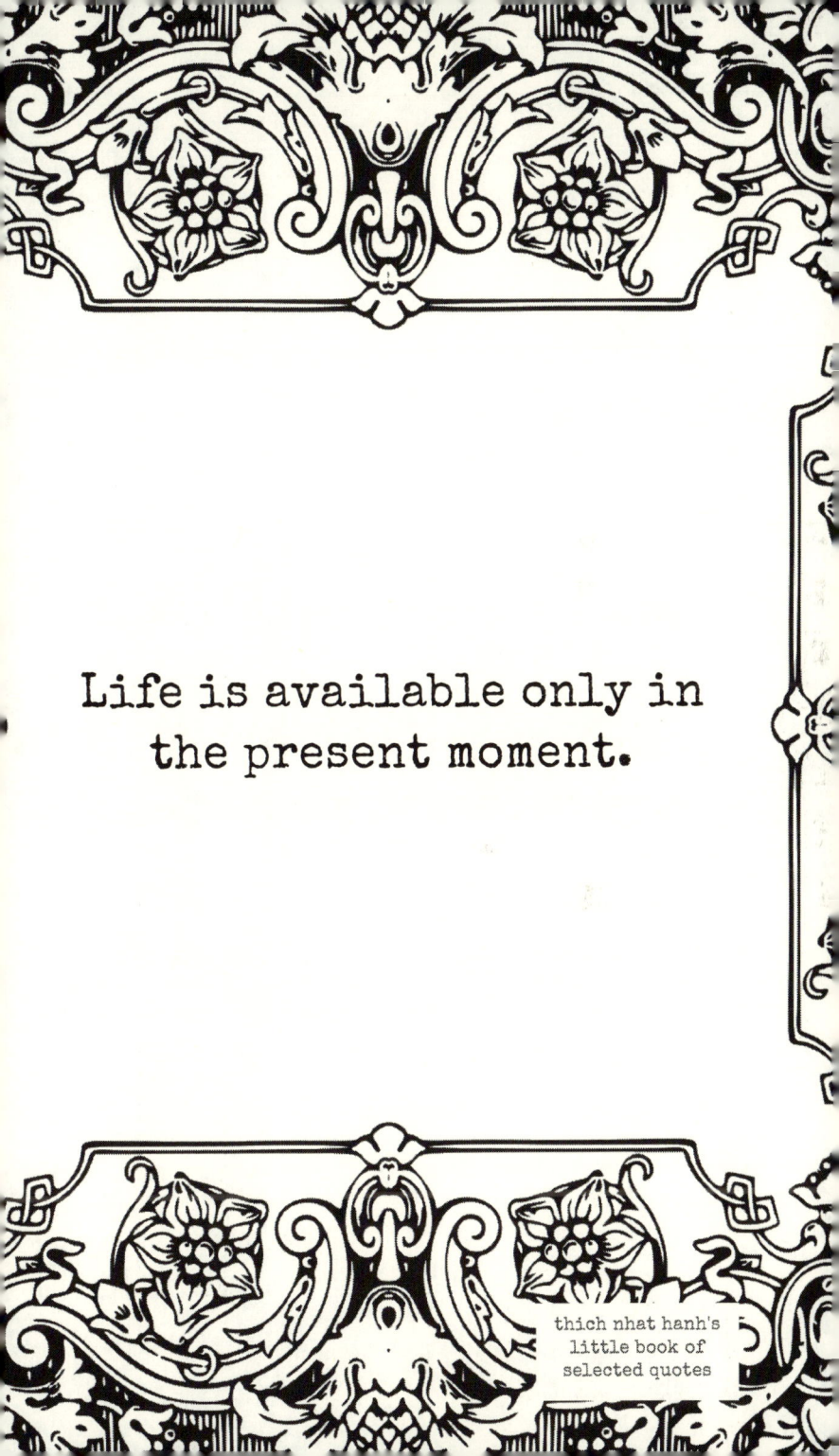

thich nhat hanh's
little book of
selected quotes

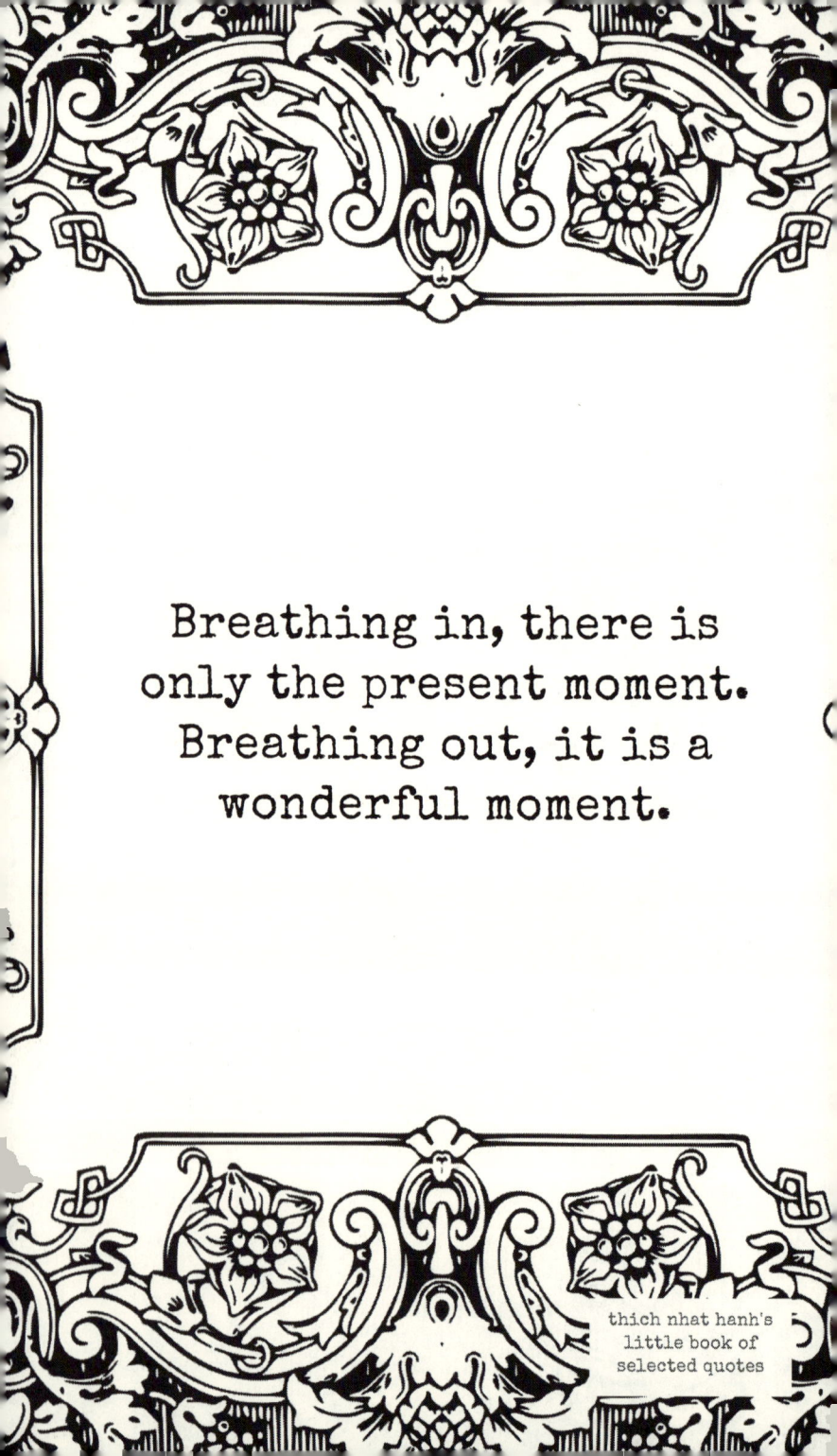

Breathing in, there is only the present moment. Breathing out, it is a wonderful moment.

thich nhat hanh's little book of selected quotes

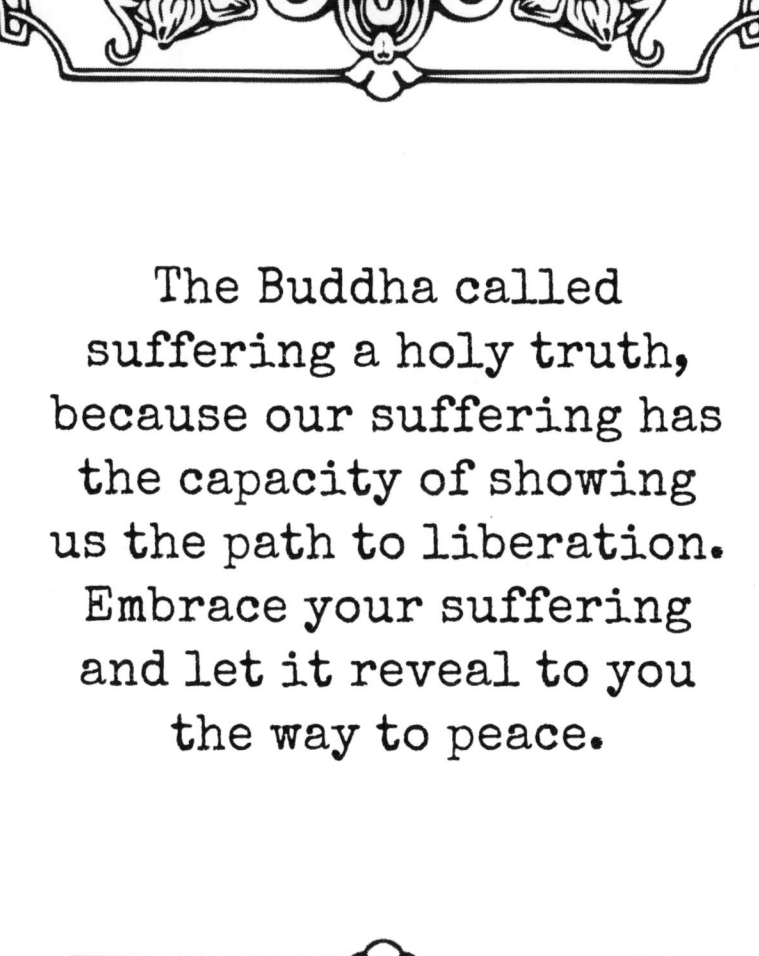

The Buddha called suffering a holy truth, because our suffering has the capacity of showing us the path to liberation. Embrace your suffering and let it reveal to you the way to peace.

thich nhat hanh's little book of selected quotes

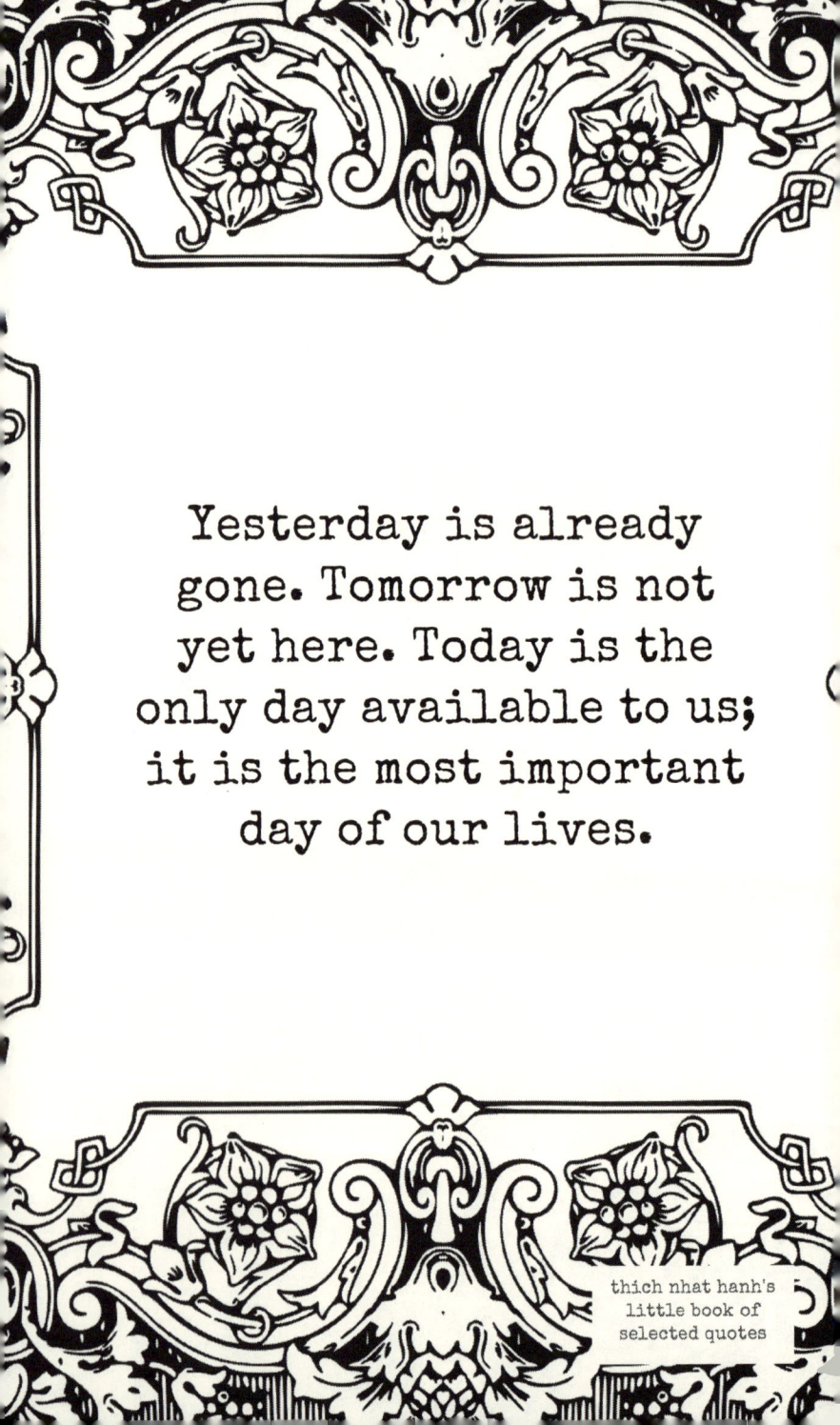

Yesterday is already gone. Tomorrow is not yet here. Today is the only day available to us; it is the most important day of our lives.

thich nhat hanh's little book of selected quotes

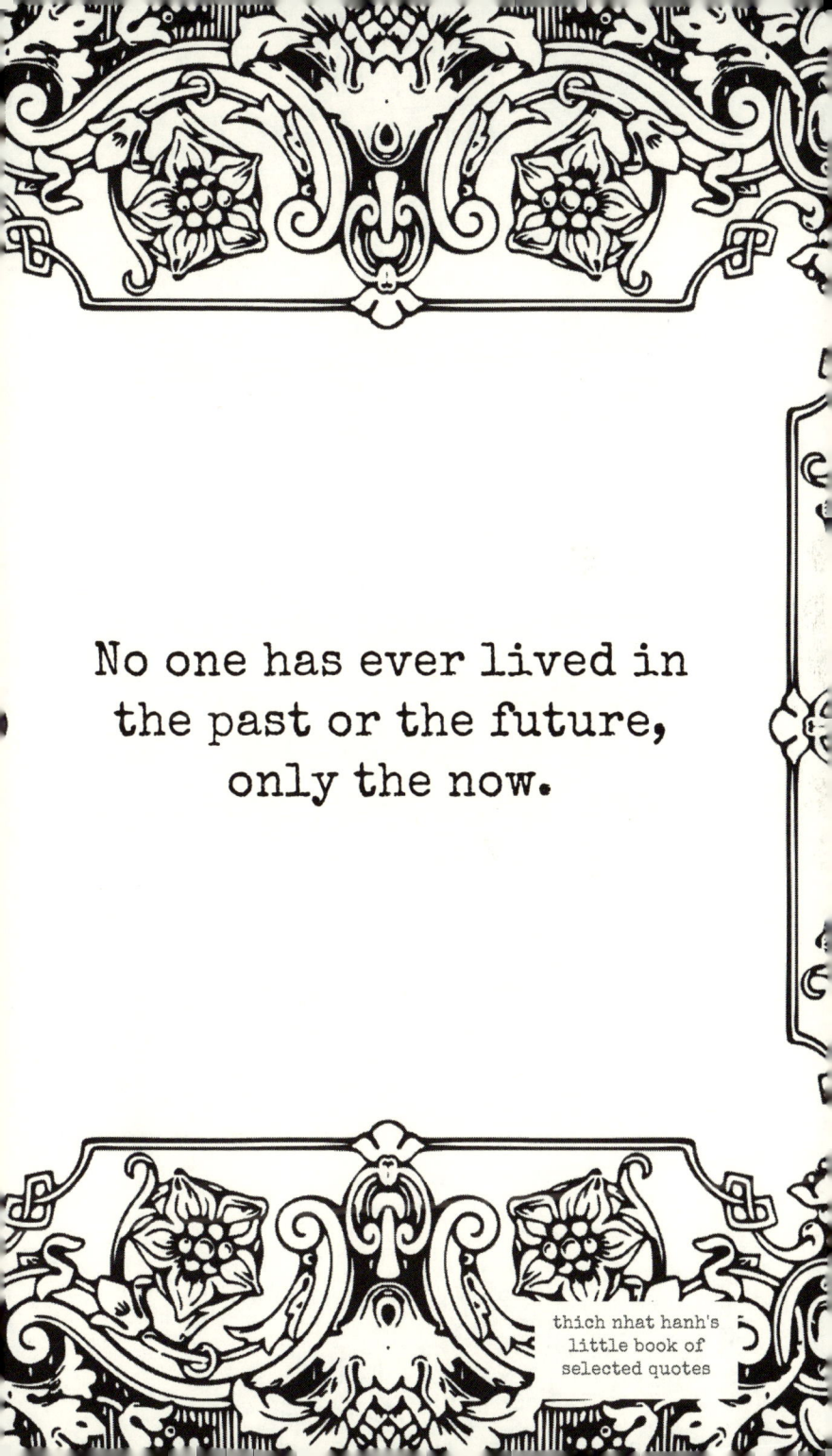

No one has ever lived in the past or the future, only the now.

thich nhat hanh's little book of selected quotes

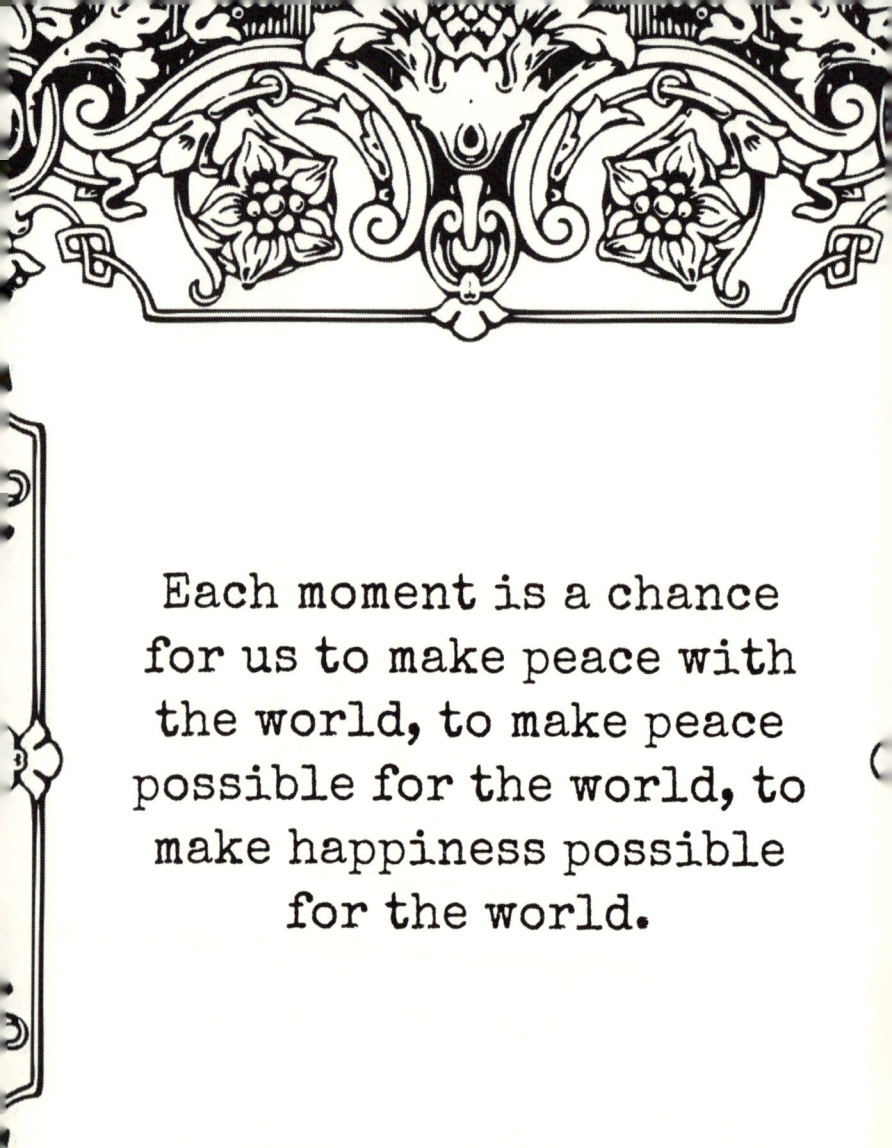

Each moment is a chance for us to make peace with the world, to make peace possible for the world, to make happiness possible for the world.

thich nhat hanh's little book of selected quotes

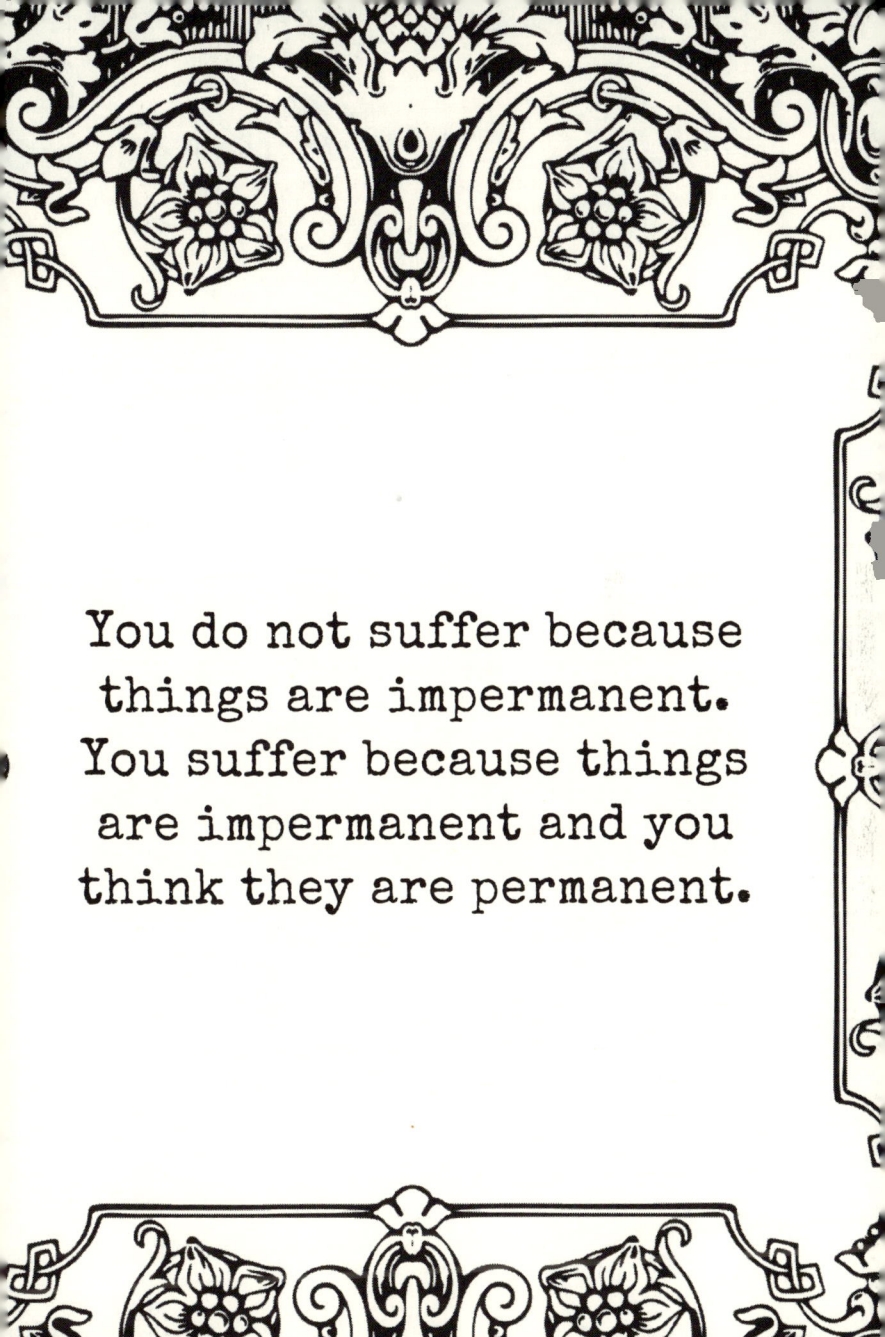

You do not suffer because things are impermanent. You suffer because things are impermanent and you think they are permanent.

thich nhat hanh's little book of selected quotes

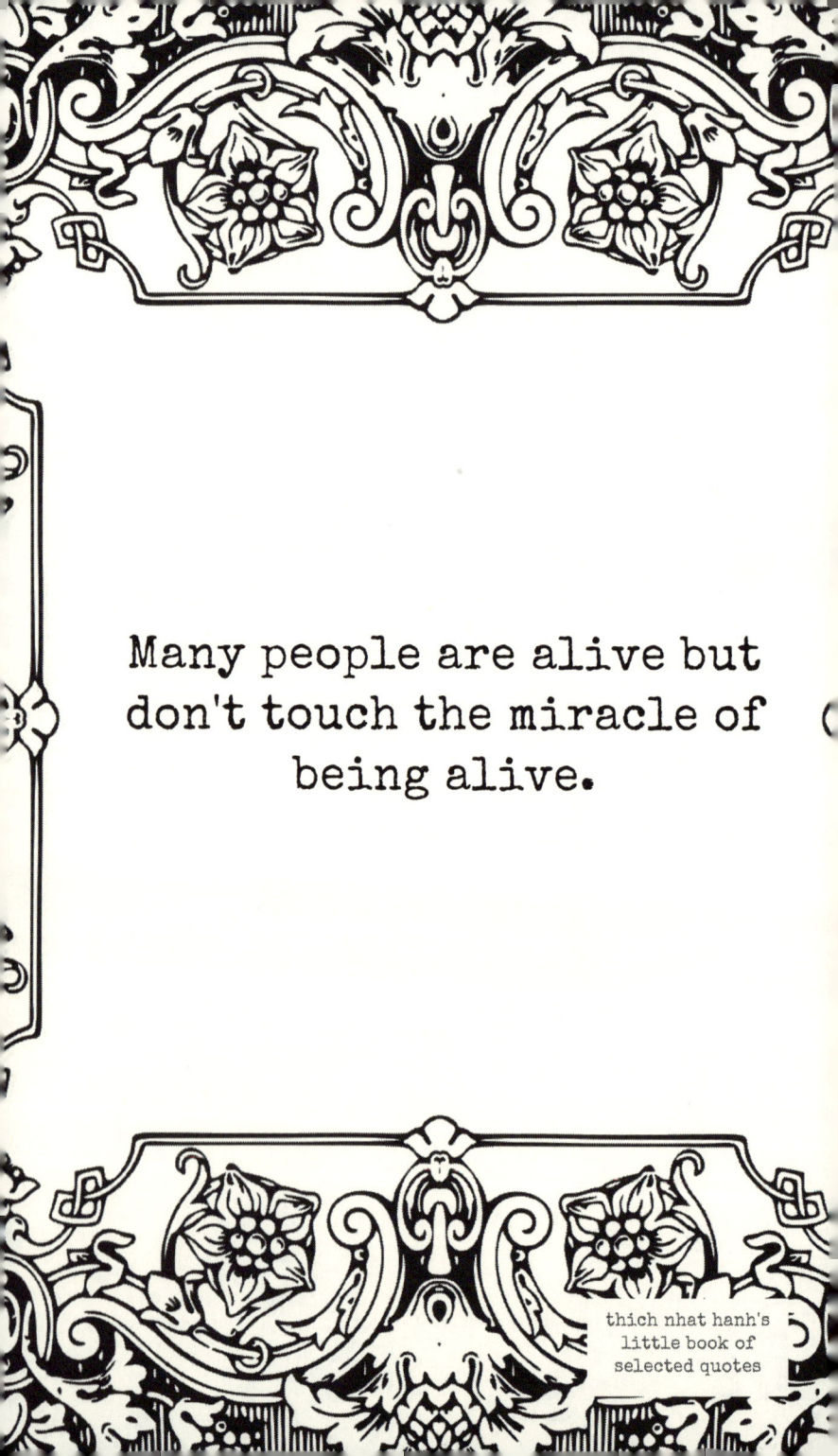

Many people are alive but don't touch the miracle of being alive.

thich nhat hanh's little book of selected quotes

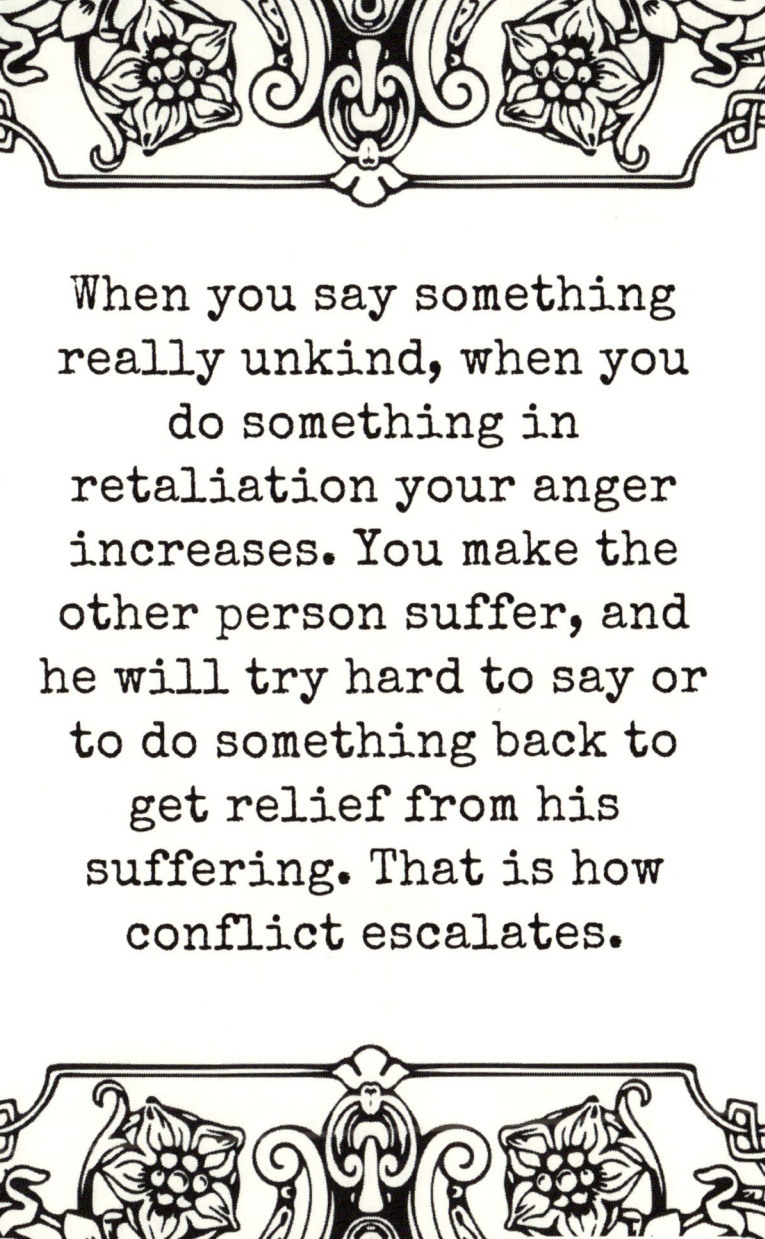

When you say something really unkind, when you do something in retaliation your anger increases. You make the other person suffer, and he will try hard to say or to do something back to get relief from his suffering. That is how conflict escalates.

thich nhat hanh's
little book of
selected quotes

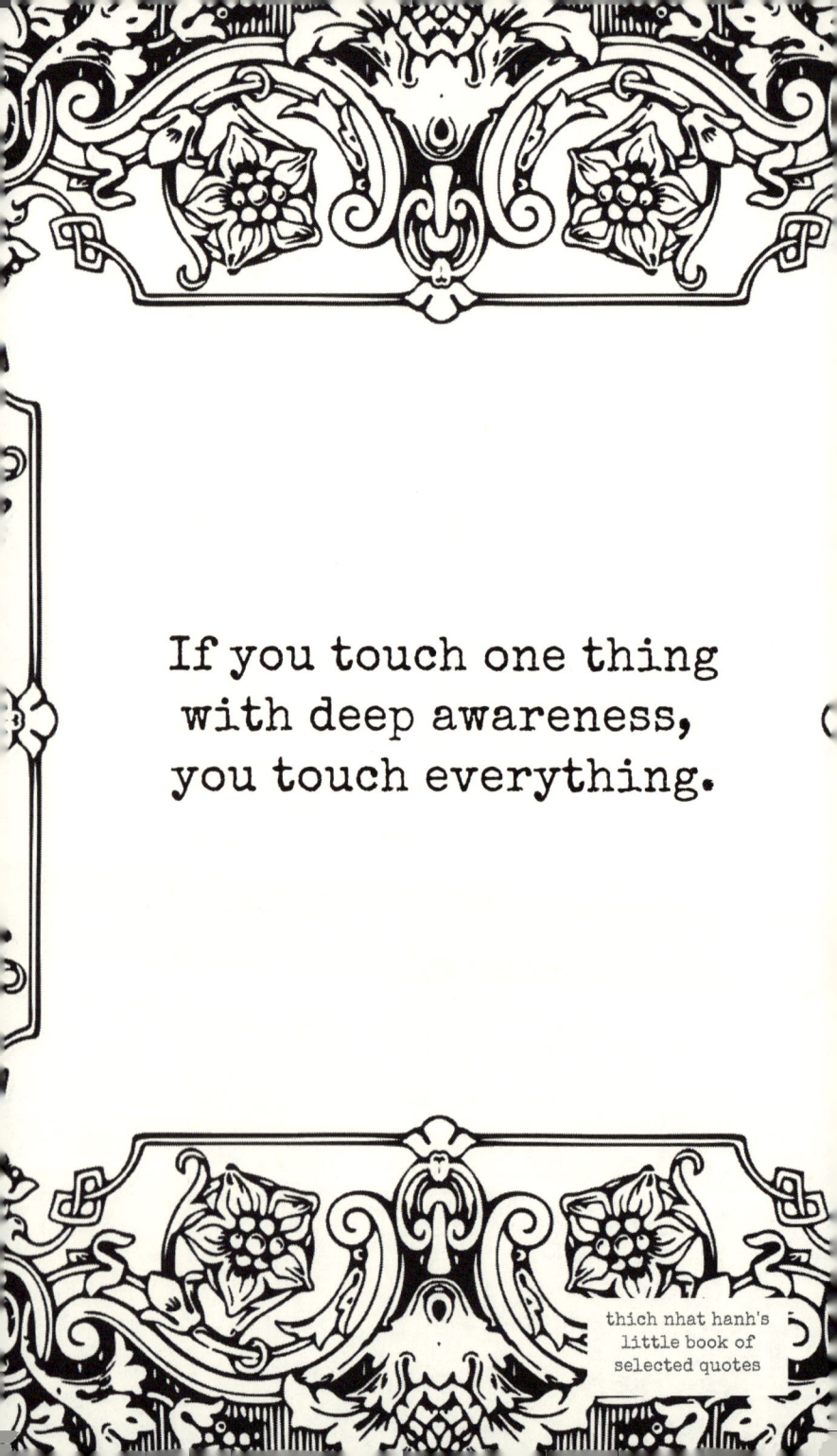

If you touch one thing
with deep awareness,
you touch everything.

thich nhat hanh's
little book of
selected quotes

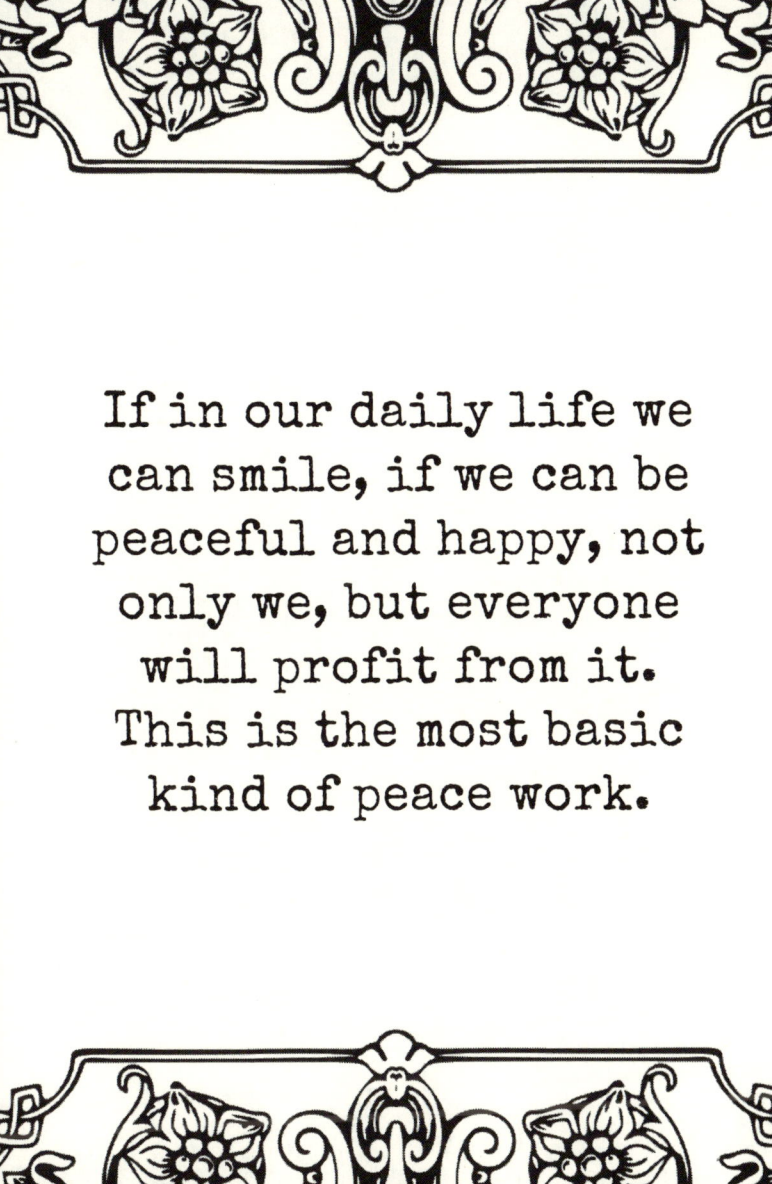

If in our daily life we can smile, if we can be peaceful and happy, not only we, but everyone will profit from it. This is the most basic kind of peace work.

thich nhat hanh's
little book of
selected quotes

In true dialogue,
both sides are
willing to change.

thich nhat hanh's
little book of
selected quotes

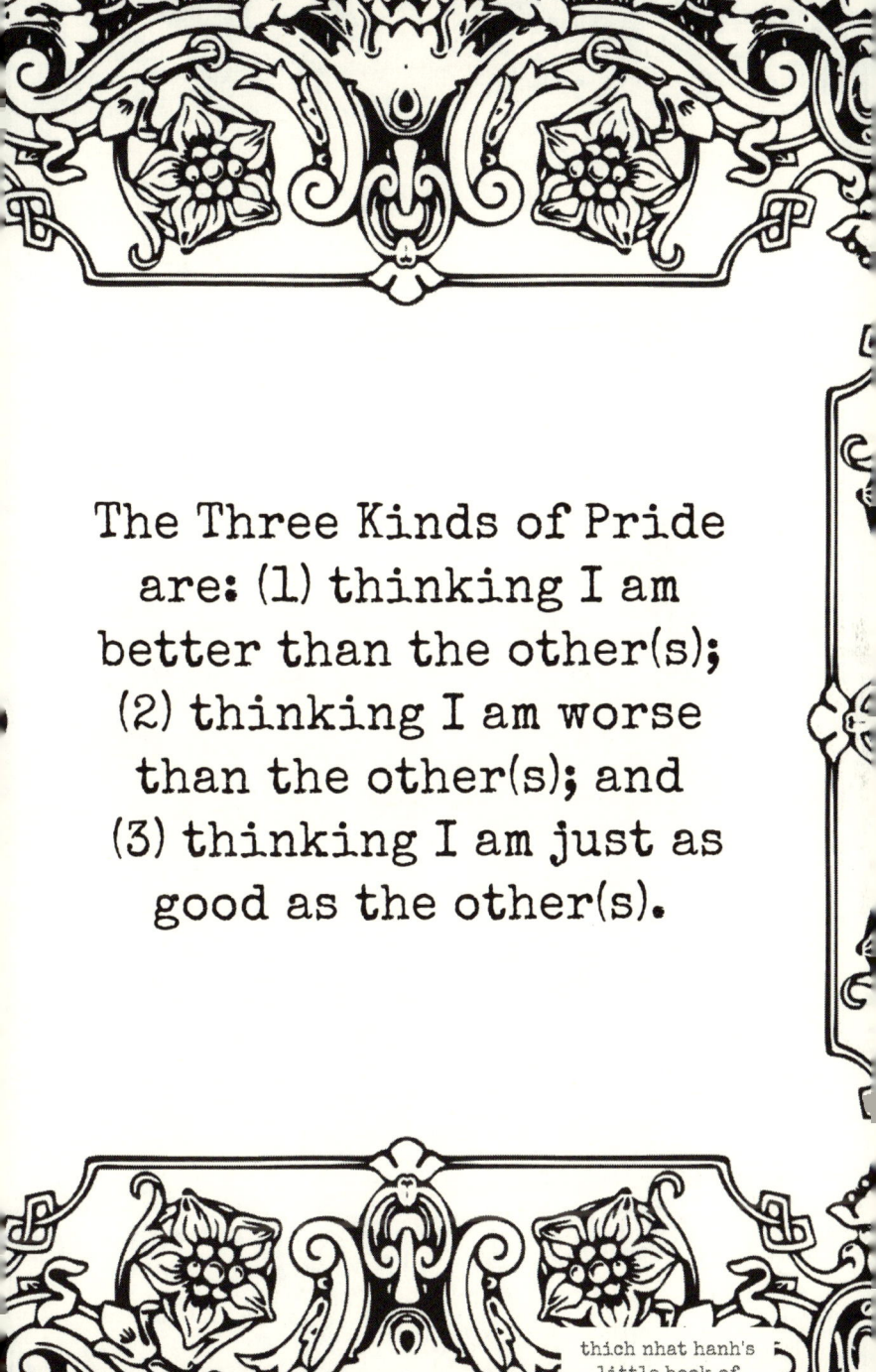

The Three Kinds of Pride are: (1) thinking I am better than the other(s); (2) thinking I am worse than the other(s); and (3) thinking I am just as good as the other(s).

thich nhat hanh's little book of selected quotes

The quality of our life depends on the quality of the seeds that lie deep in our consciousness.

thich nhat hanh's little book of selected quotes

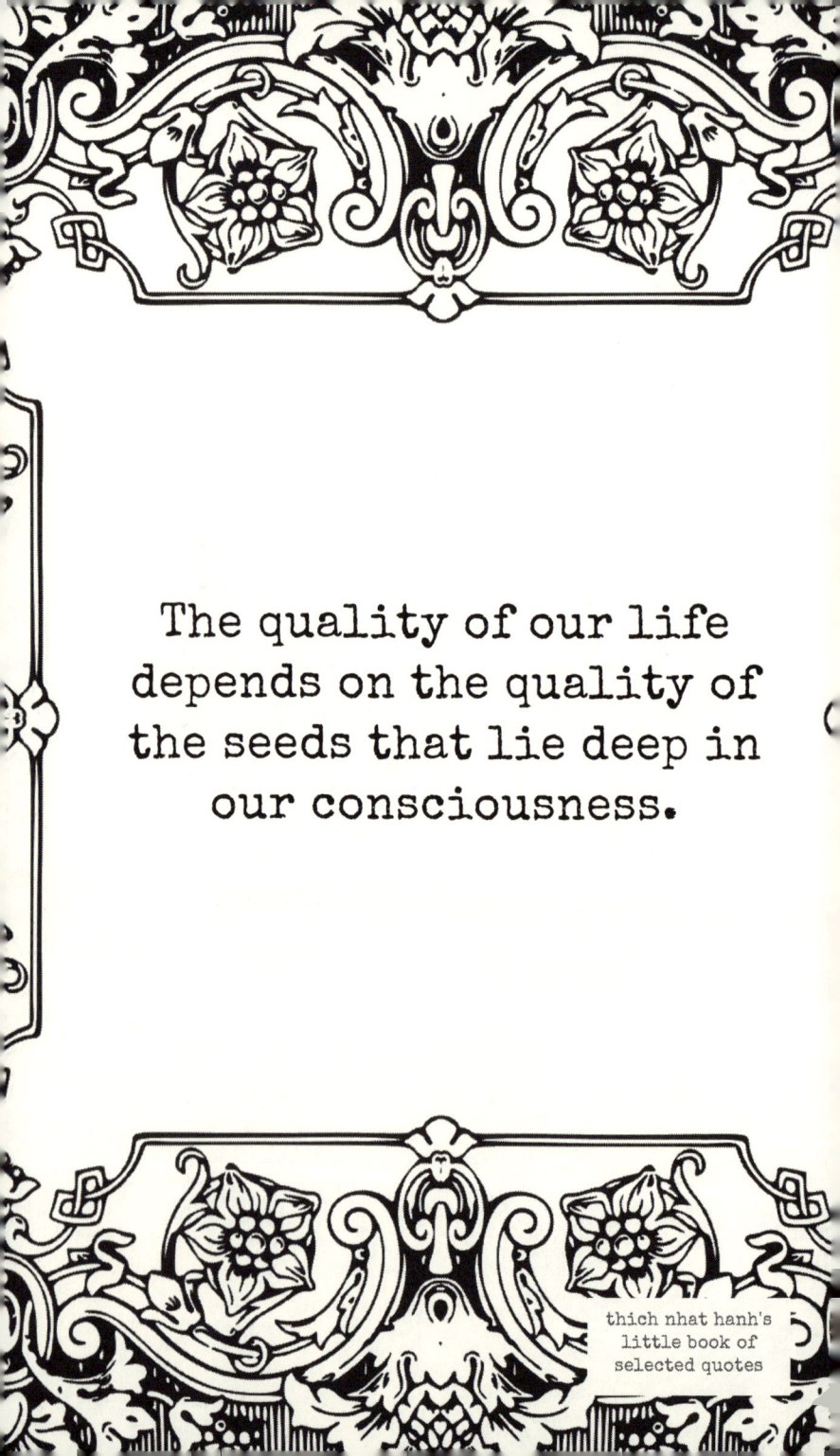

It is possible to live twenty-four hours a day in a state of love. Every movement, every glance, every thought, and every word can be infused with love.

thich nhat hanh's little book of selected quotes

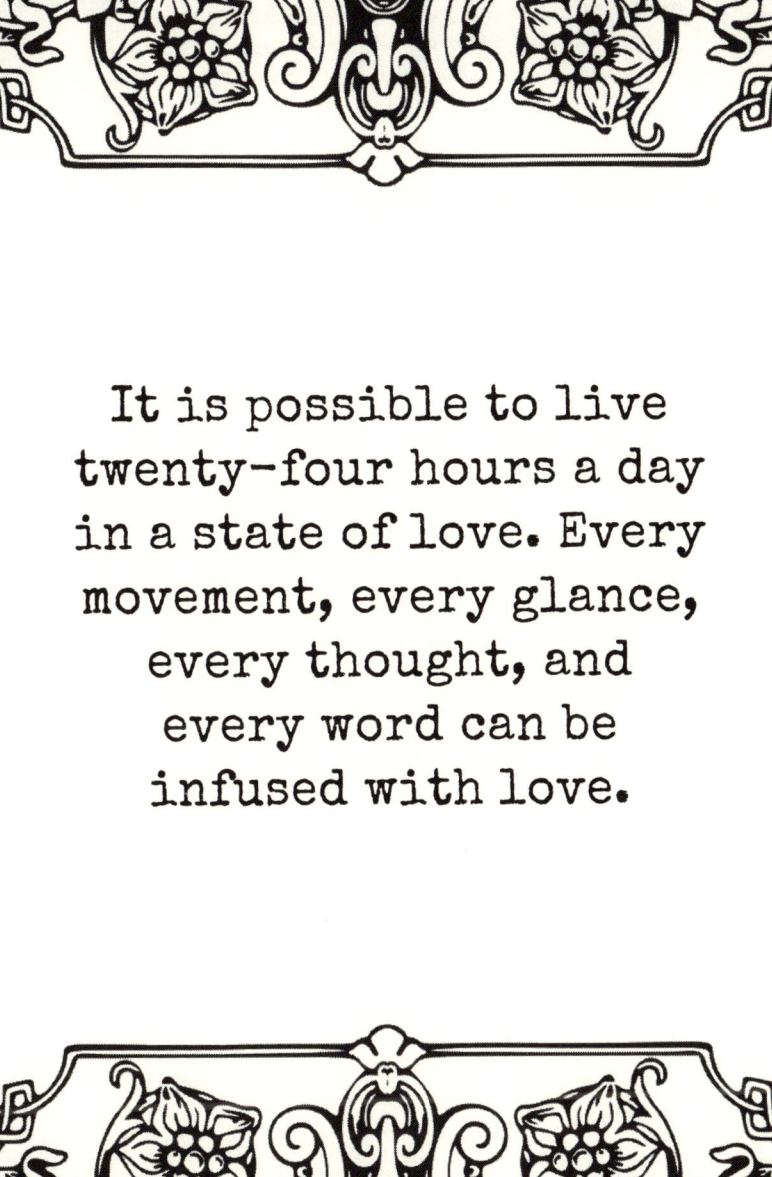

The way you speak to others can offer them joy, happiness, self-confidence, hope, trust, and enlightenment. Mindful speaking is a deep practice.

thich nhat hanh's little book of selected quotes

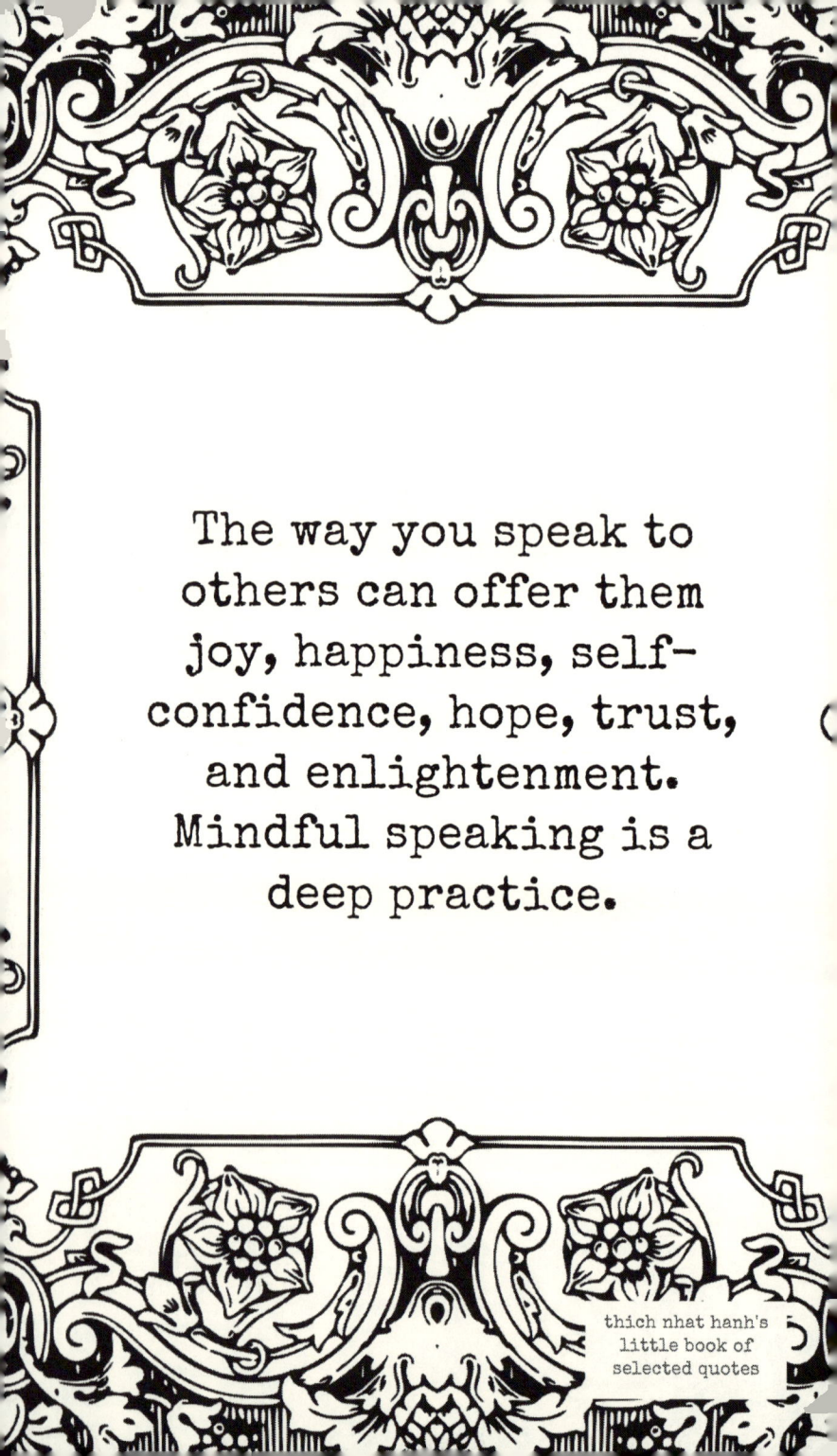

Our notions about happiness entrap us. We forget that they are just ideas. Our idea of happiness can prevent us from actually being happy.
We fail to see the opportunity for joy that is right in front of us when we are caught in a belief that happiness should take a particular form.

thich nhat hanh's little book of selected quotes

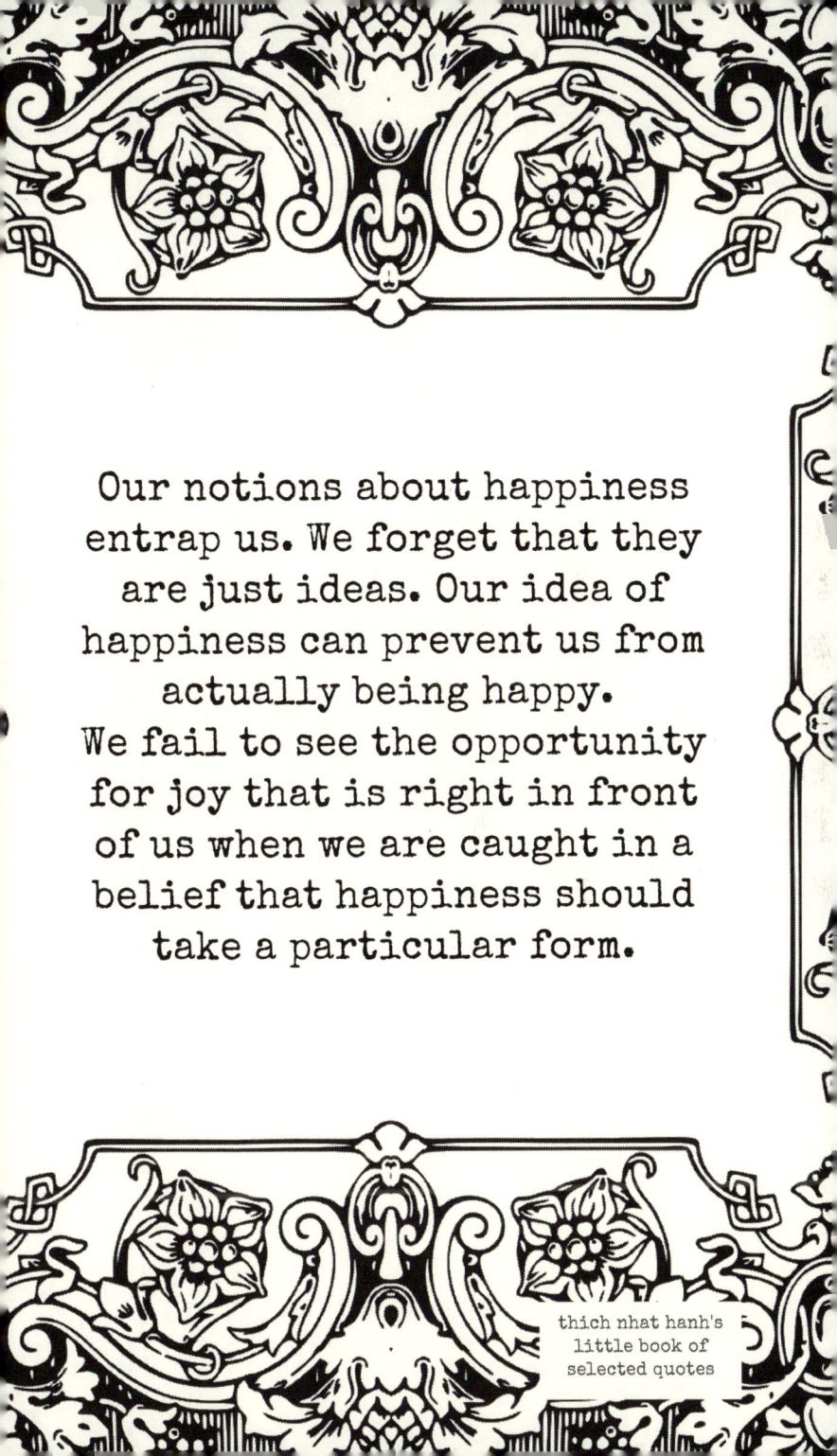

I have noticed that people are dealing too much with the negative, with what is wrong. ... Why not try the other way, to look into the patient and see positive things, to just touch those things and make them bloom?

thich nhat hanh's little book of selected quotes

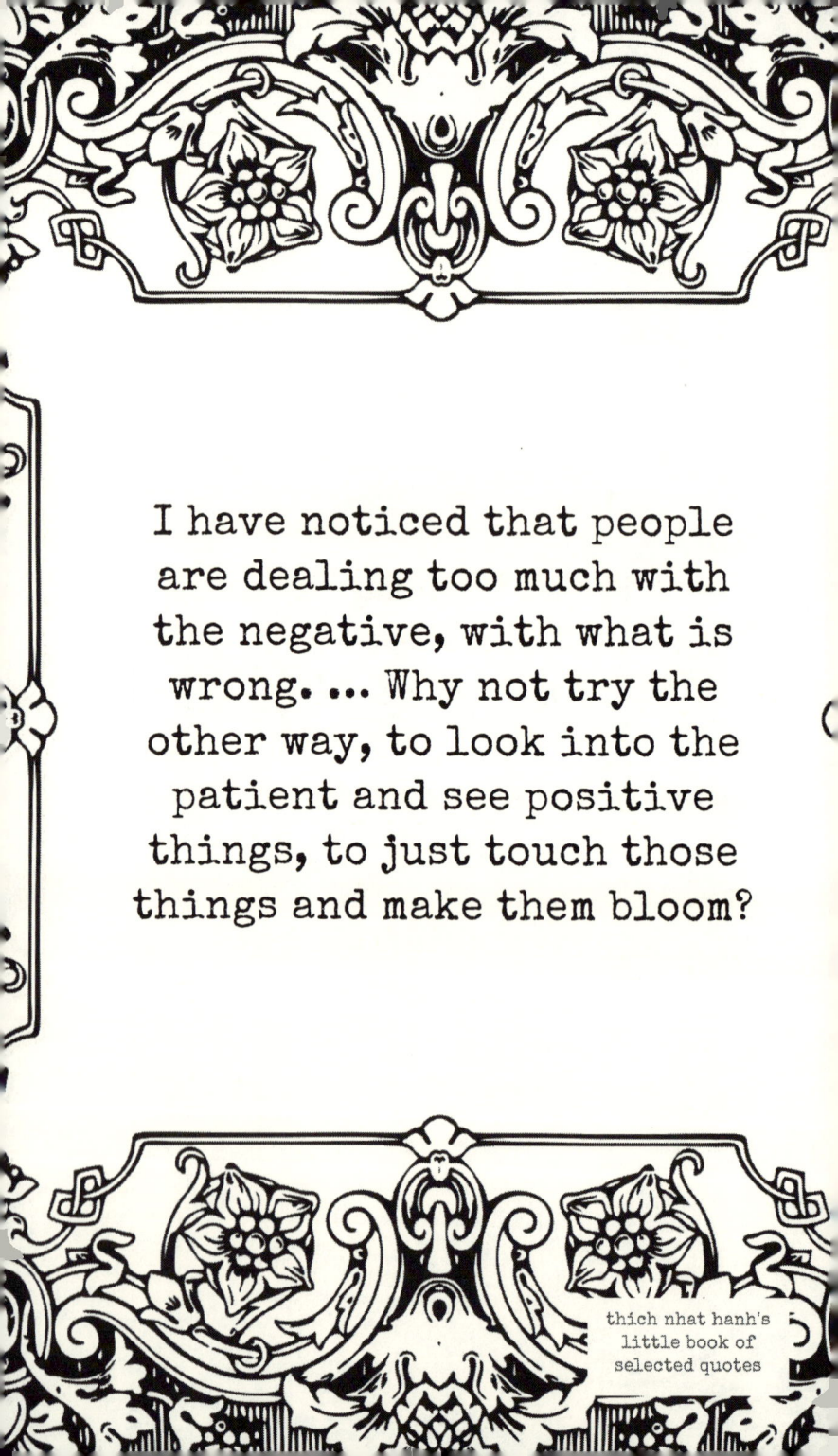

Some people live as though they are already dead. There are people moving around us who are consumed by their past, terrified of their future, and stuck in their anger and jealousy. They are not alive; they are just walking corpses.

thich nhat hanh's little book of selected quotes

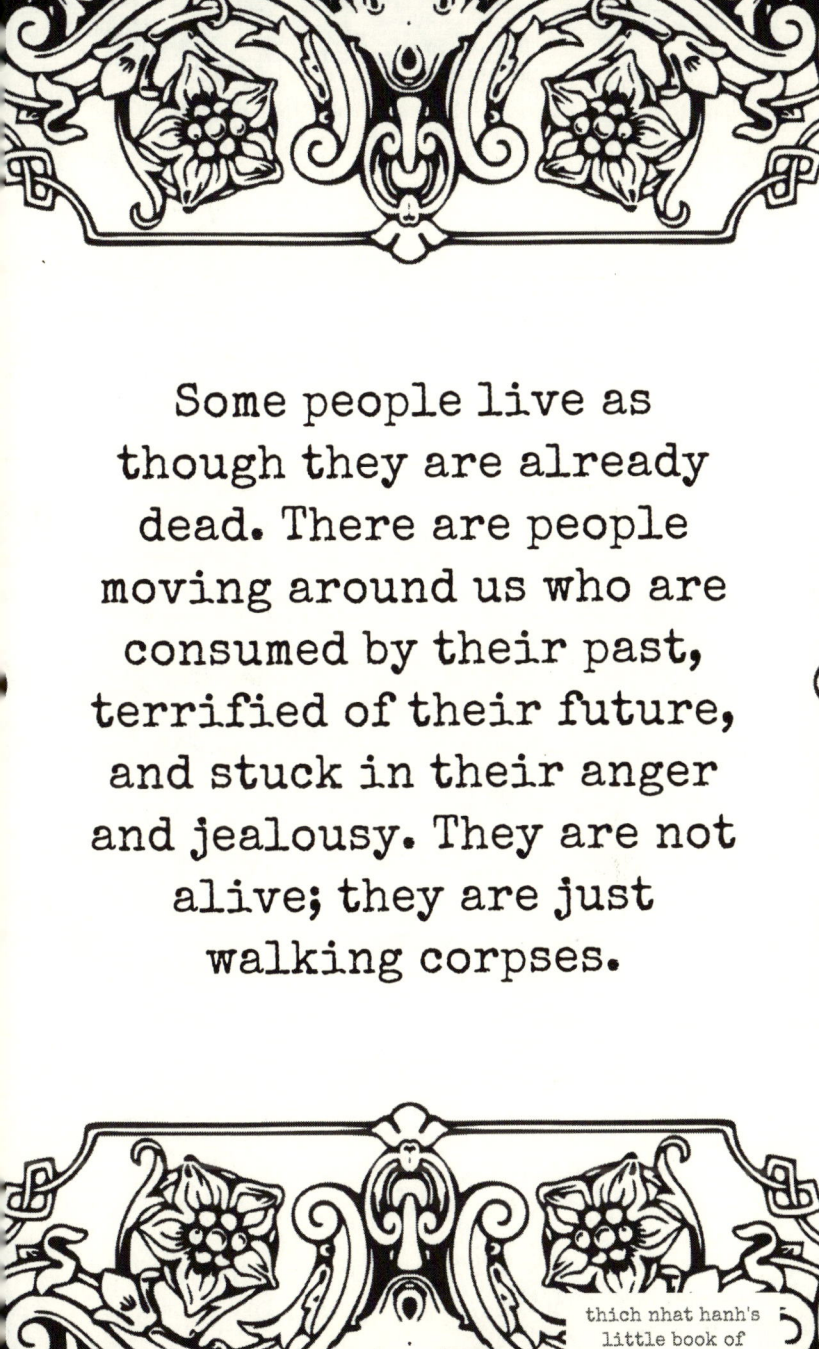

Be Yourself. Life is precious as it is. All the elements for your happiness are already here. There is no need to run, strive, search, or struggle. Just Be.

thich nhat hanh's little book of selected quotes

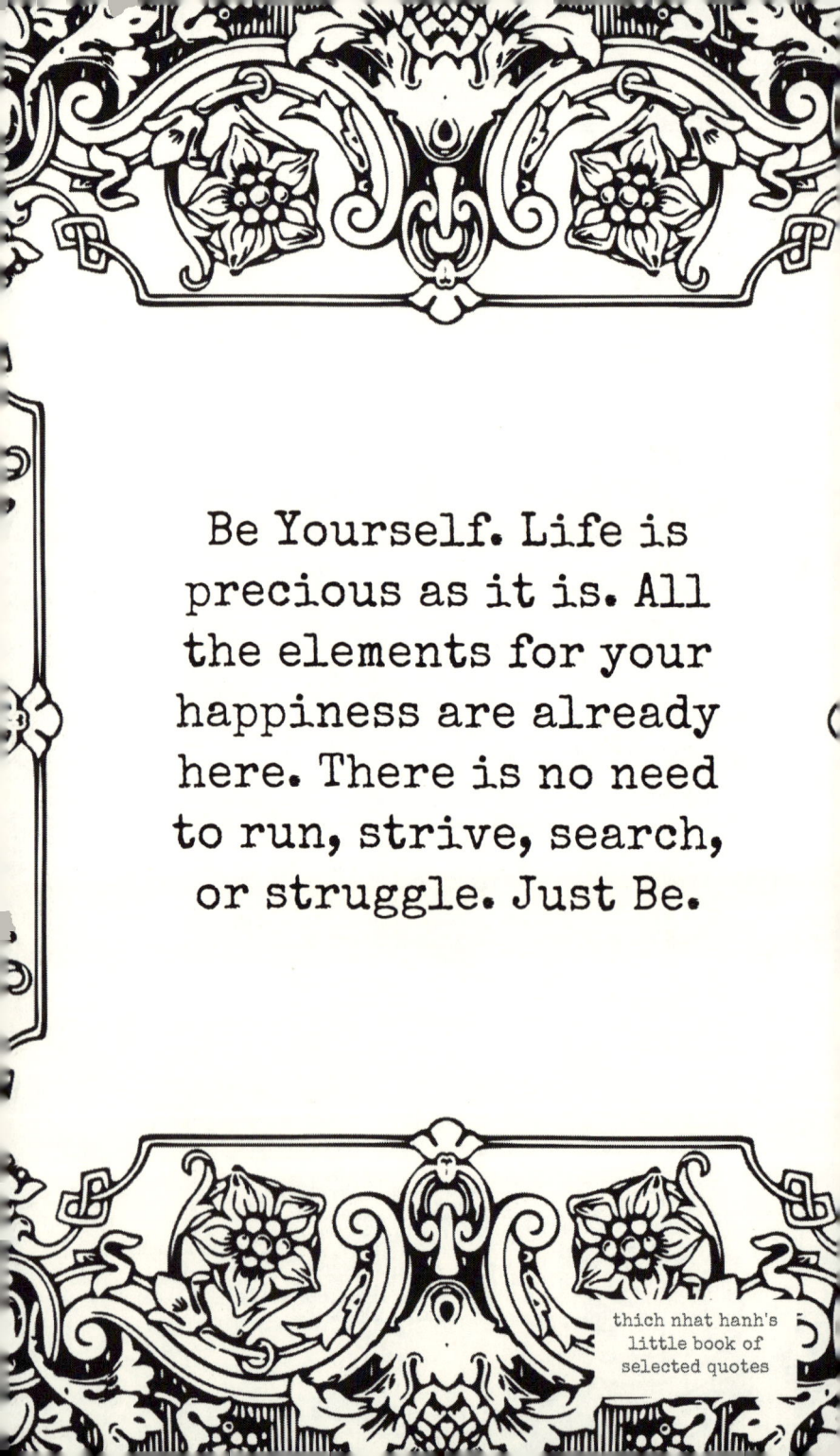

When you begin to see that your enemy is suffering, that is the beginning of insight.

thich nhat hanh's little book of selected quotes

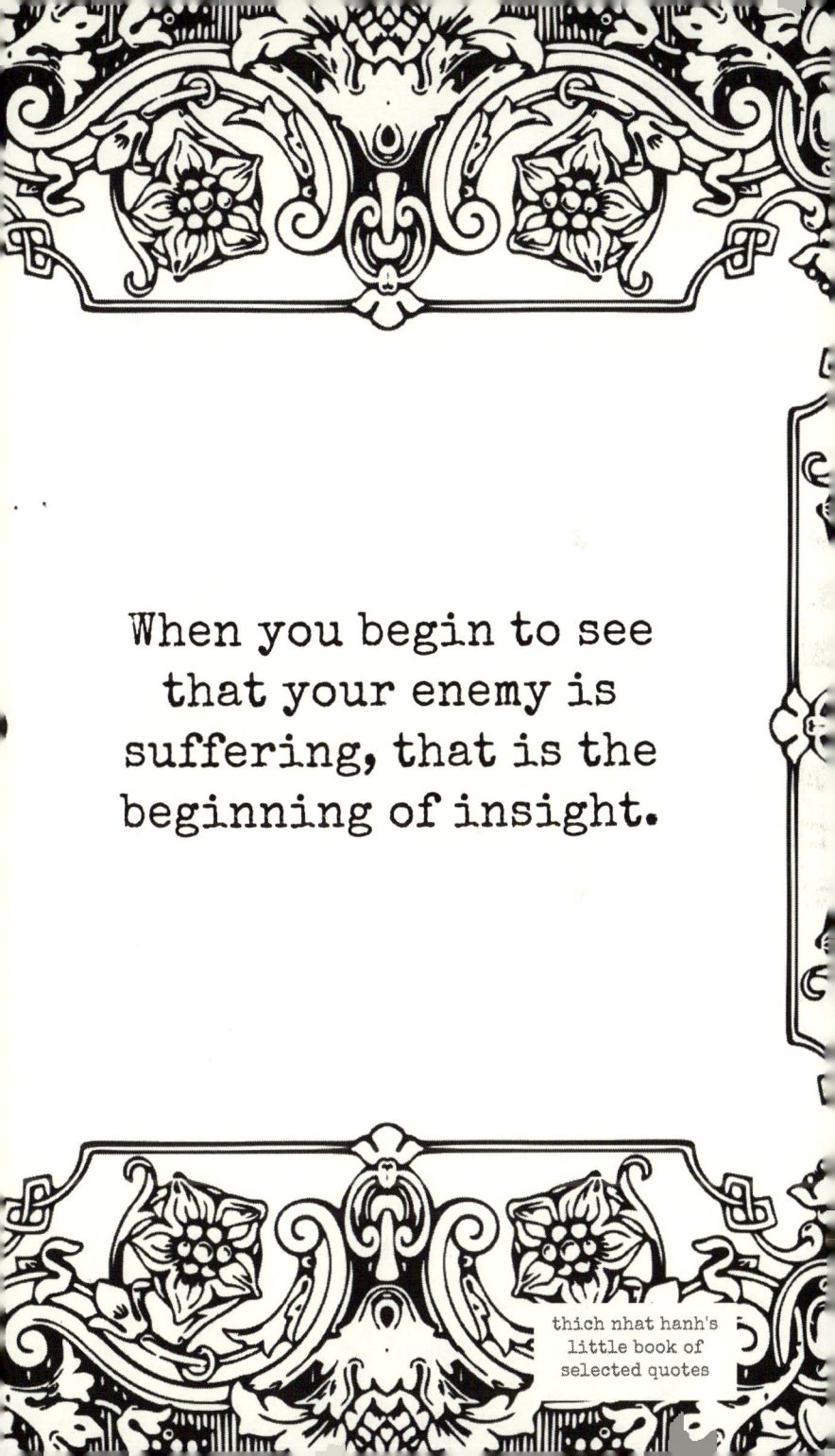

Patience is the mark of true love. If you truly love someone, you will be more patient with that person.

thich nhat hanh's little book of selected quotes

From time to time, to remind ourselves to relax and be peaceful, we may wish to set aside some time for a retreat, a day of mindfulness, when we can walk slowly, smile, drink tea with a friend, enjoy being together as if we are the happiest people on Earth.

thich nhat hanh's little book of selected quotes

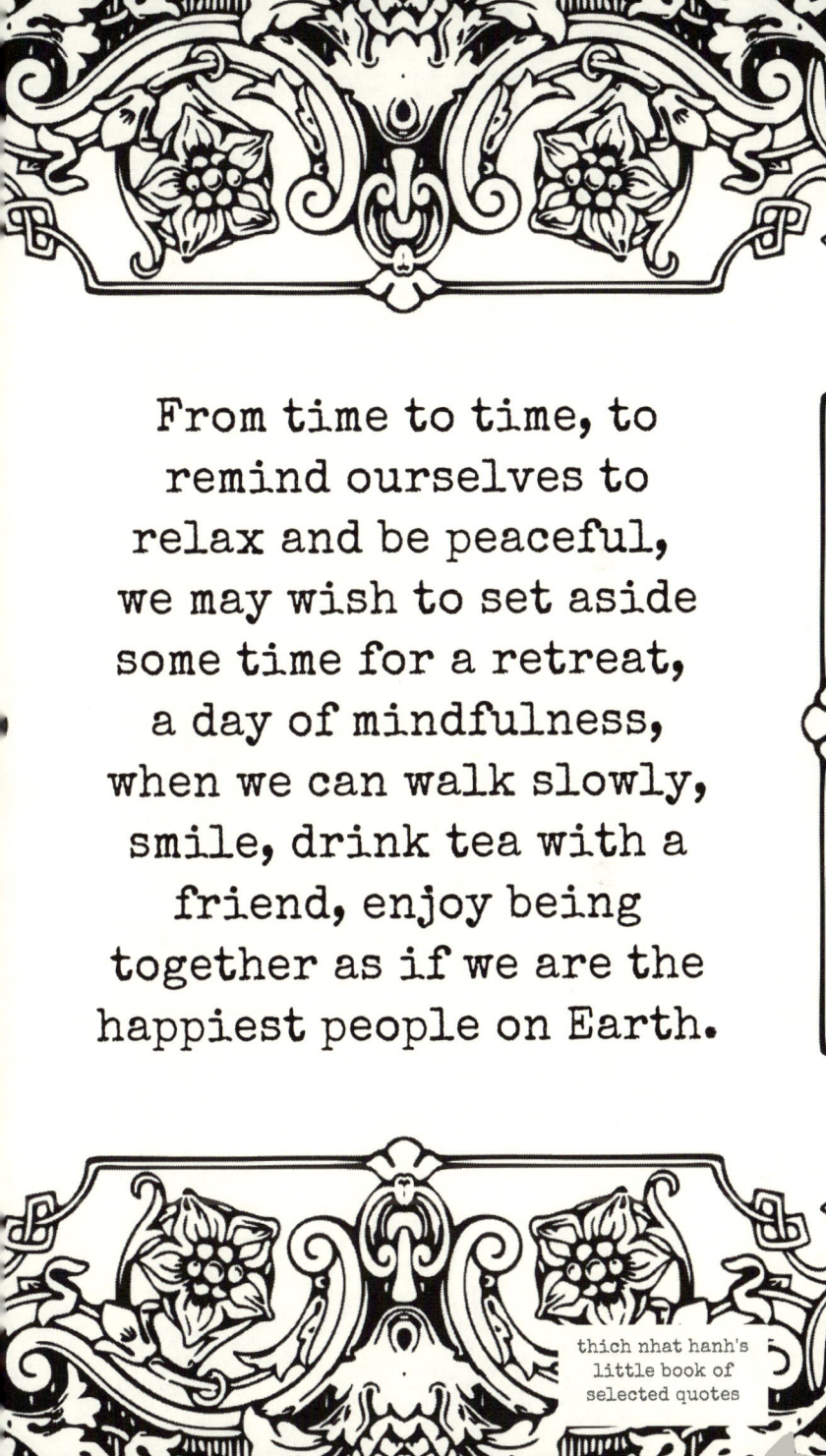

I promise myself that I will enjoy every minute of the day that is given me to live.

thich nhat hanh's little book of selected quotes

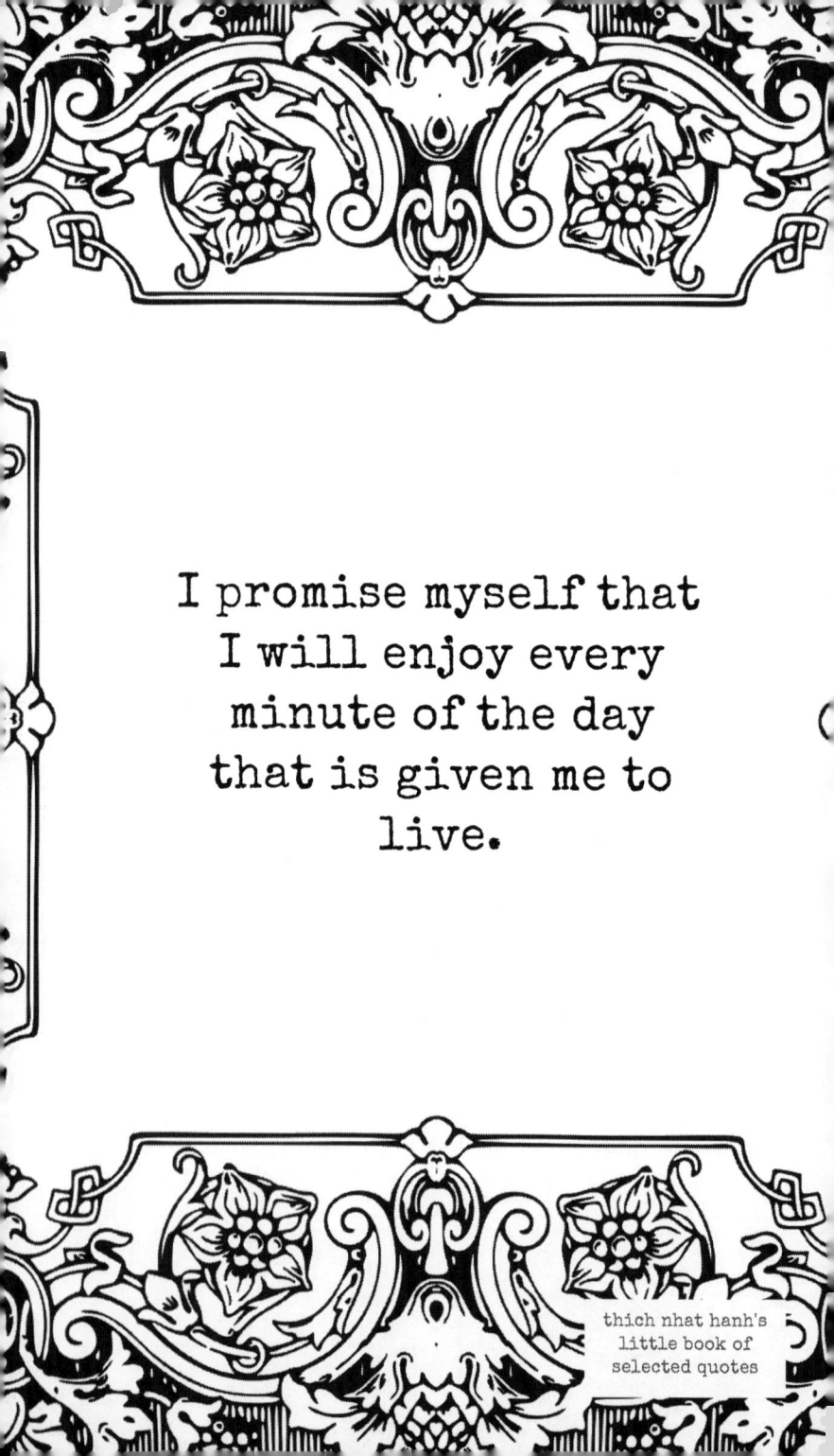

Look at flowers,
butterflies, trees,
and children with the
eyes of compassion.
Compassion will
change your life and
make it wonderful.

thich nhat hanh's
little book of
selected quotes

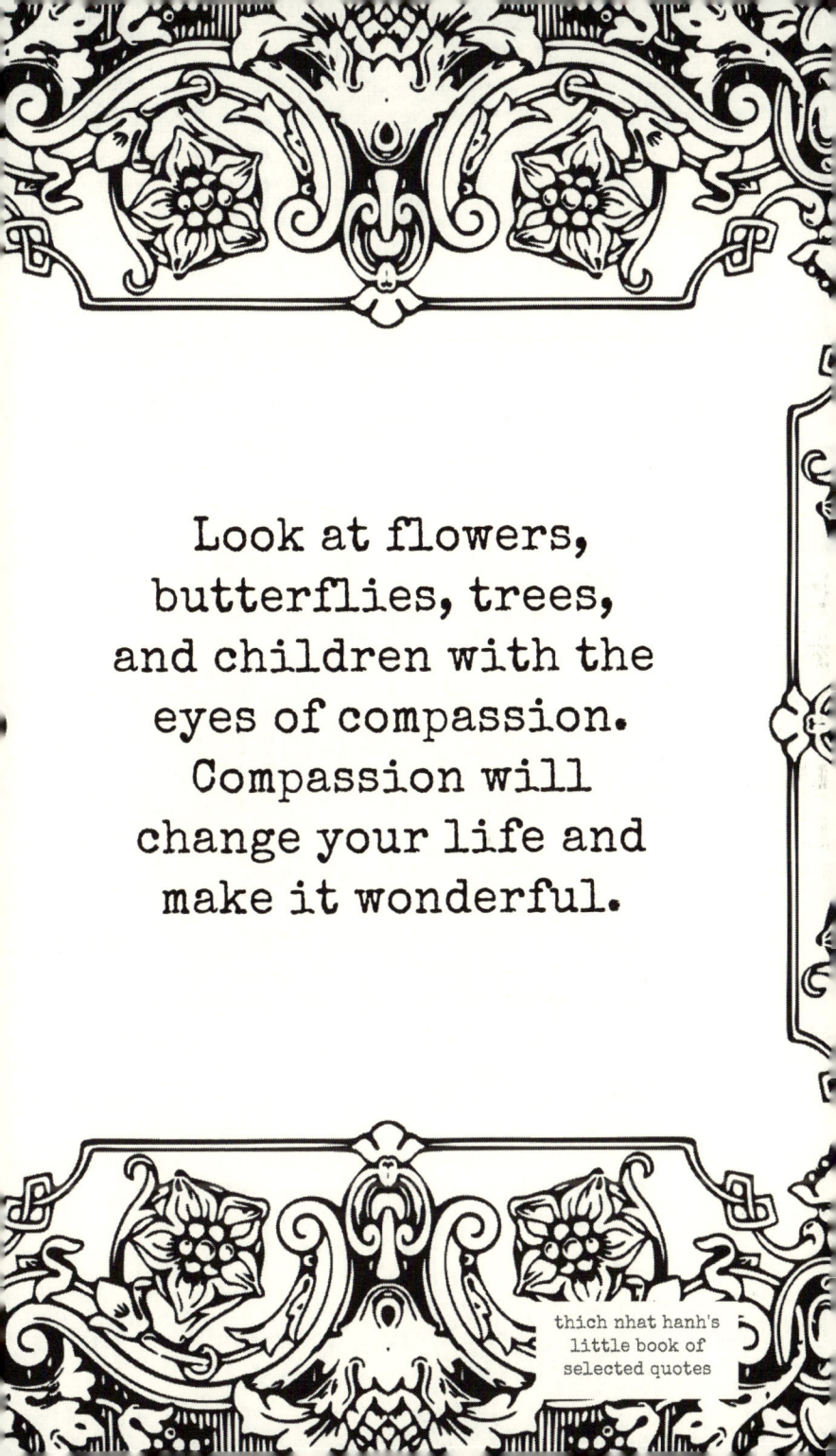

We will be more successful in all our endeavors if we can let go of the habit of running all the time, and take little pauses to relax and re-center ourselves. And we'll also have a lot more joy in living.

thich nhat hanh's little book of selected quotes

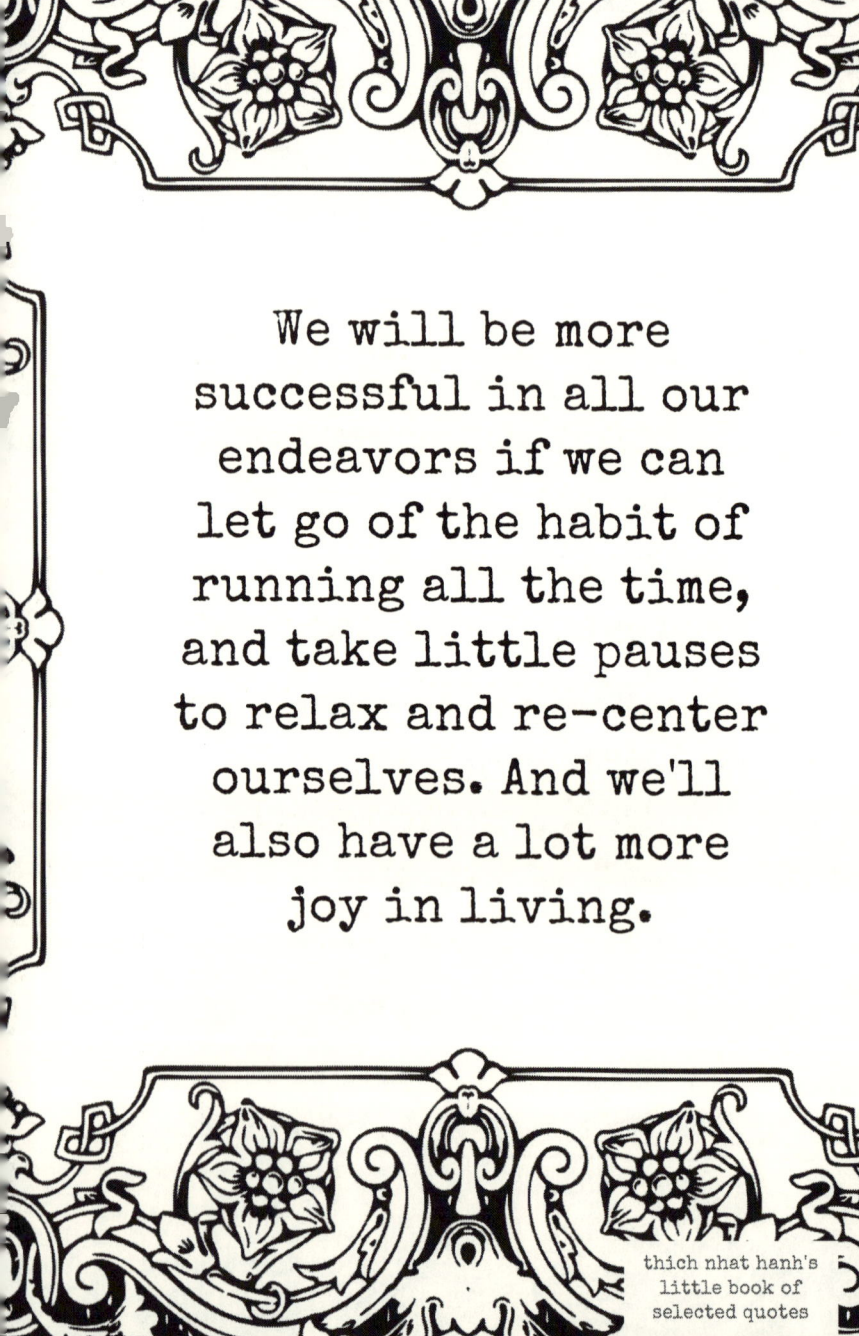

People have a hard time letting go of their suffering. Out of a fear of the unknown, they prefer suffering that is familiar.

thich nhat hanh's little book of selected quotes

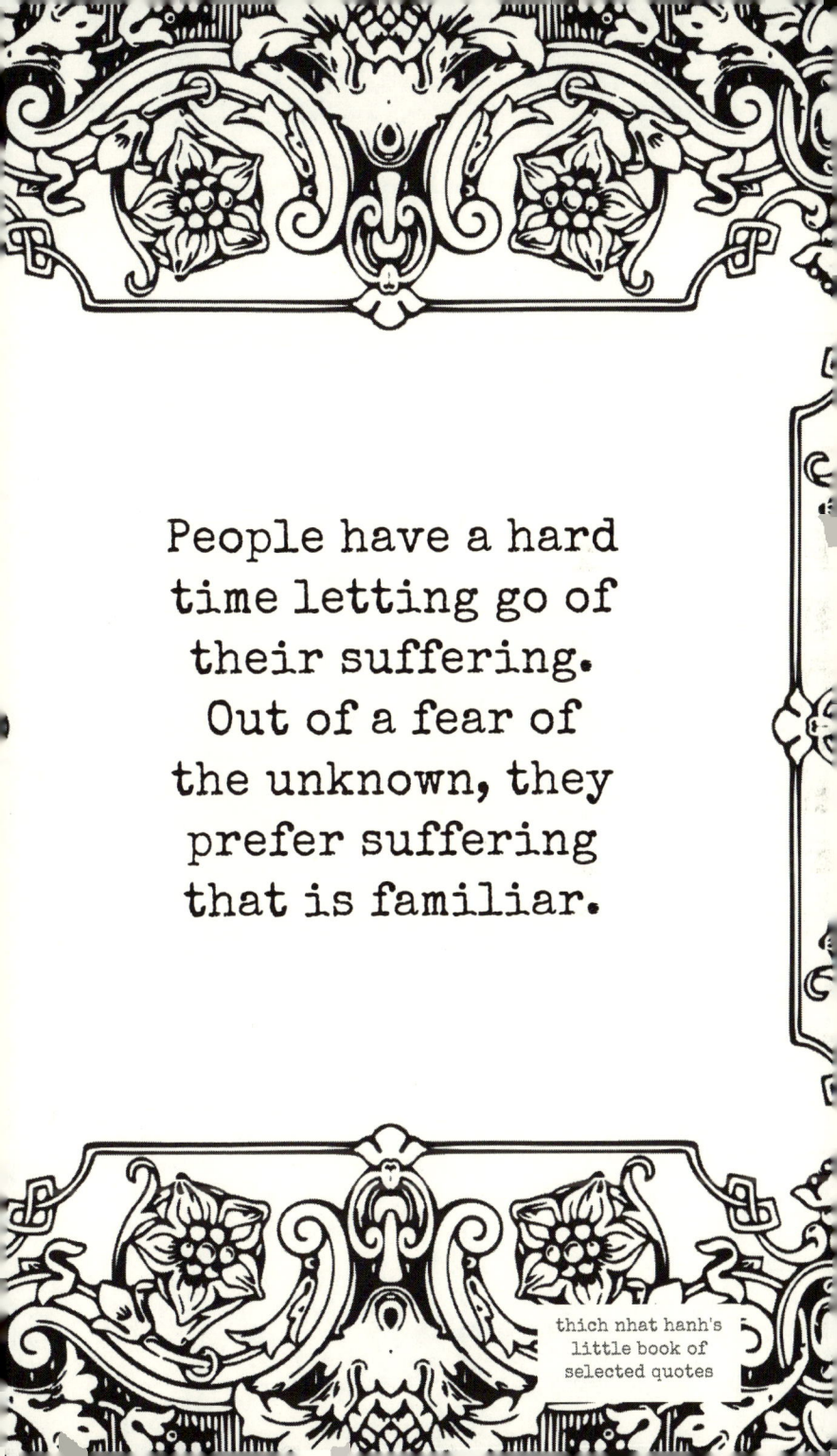

Understanding means throwing away your knowledge.

thich nhat hanh's
little book of
selected quotes

Letting go gives us freedom, and freedom is the only condition for happiness. If, in our heart, we still cling to anything – anger, anxiety, or possessions – we cannot be free.

thich nhat hanh's little book of selected quotes

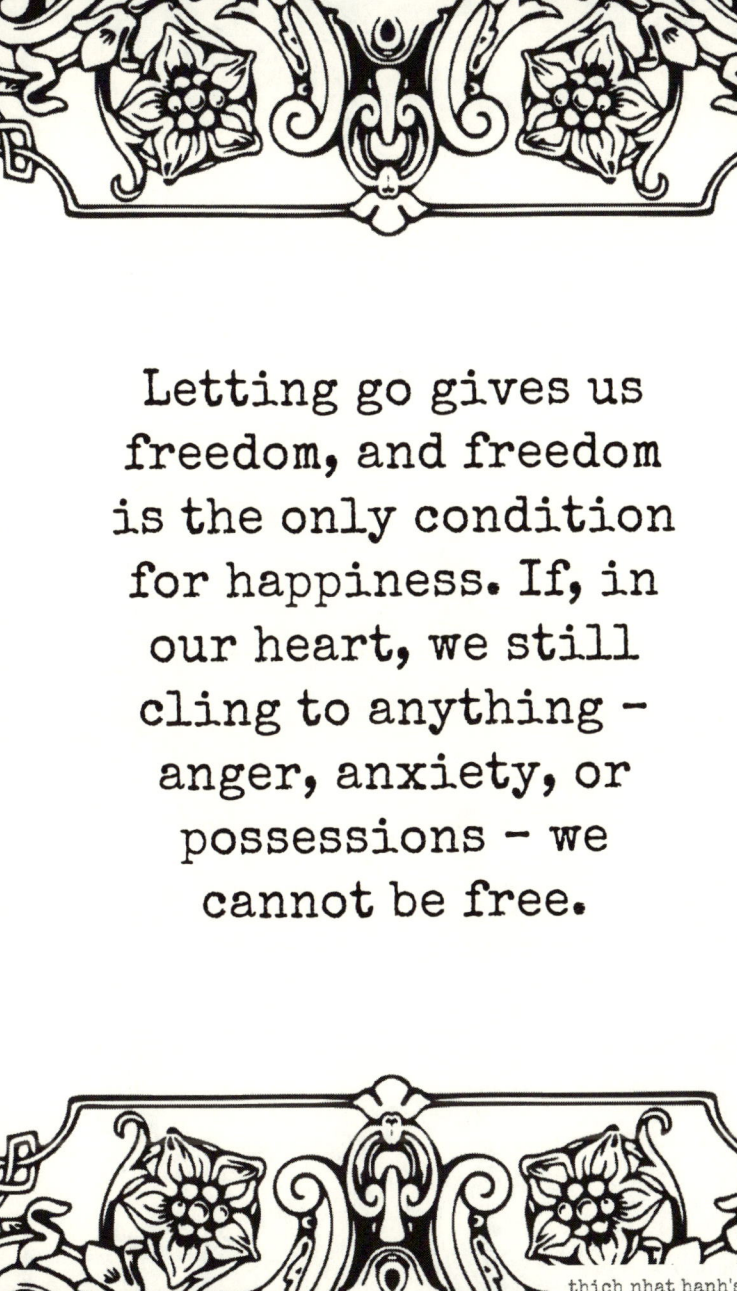

You have to learn how to help a wounded child while still practicing mindful breathing. You should not allow yourself to get lost in action. Action should be meditation at the same time.

thich nhat hanh's little book of selected quotes

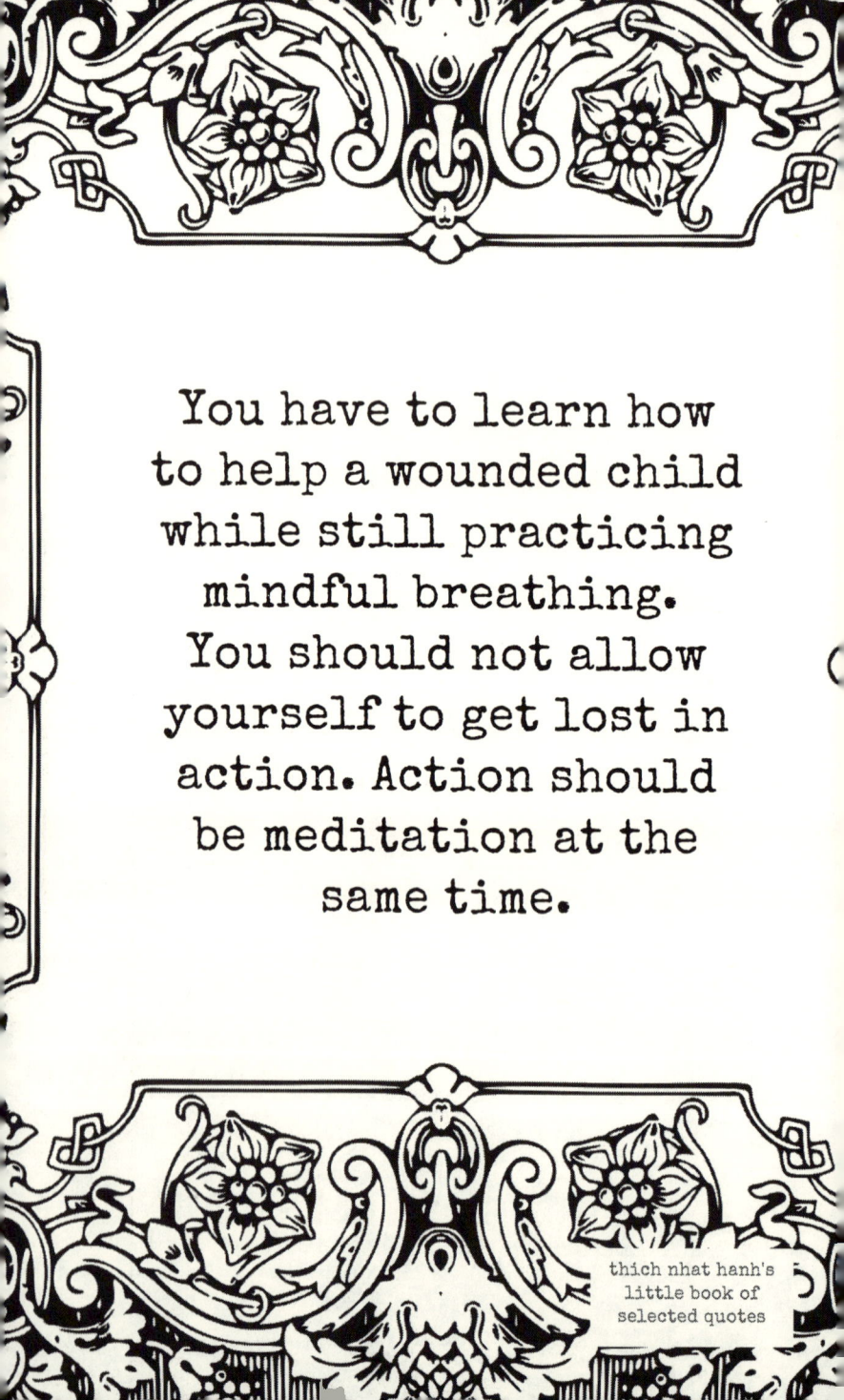

The past is gone, the future is not yet here, and if we do not go back to ourselves in the present moment, we cannot be in touch with life.

thich nhat hanh's little book of selected quotes

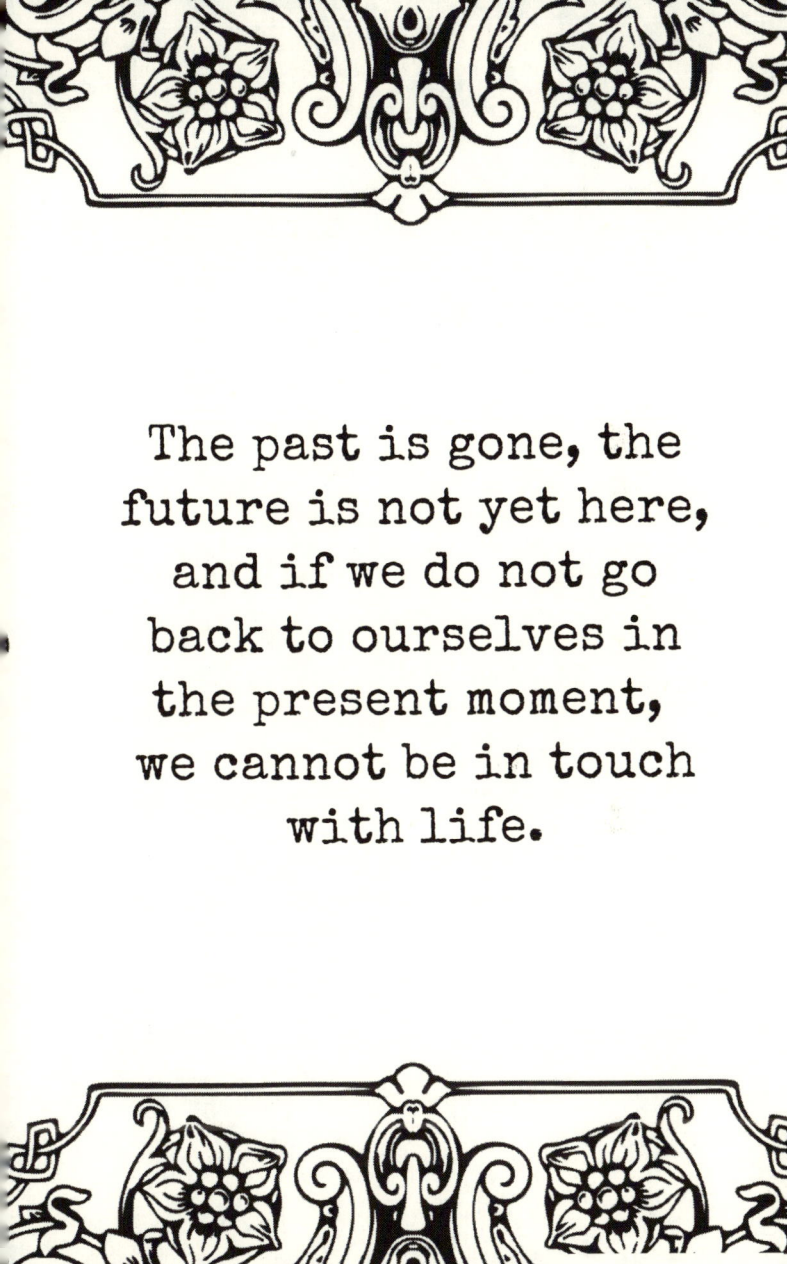

The wave does not need
to die to become water.
She is already water.

thich nhat hanh's
little book of
selected quotes

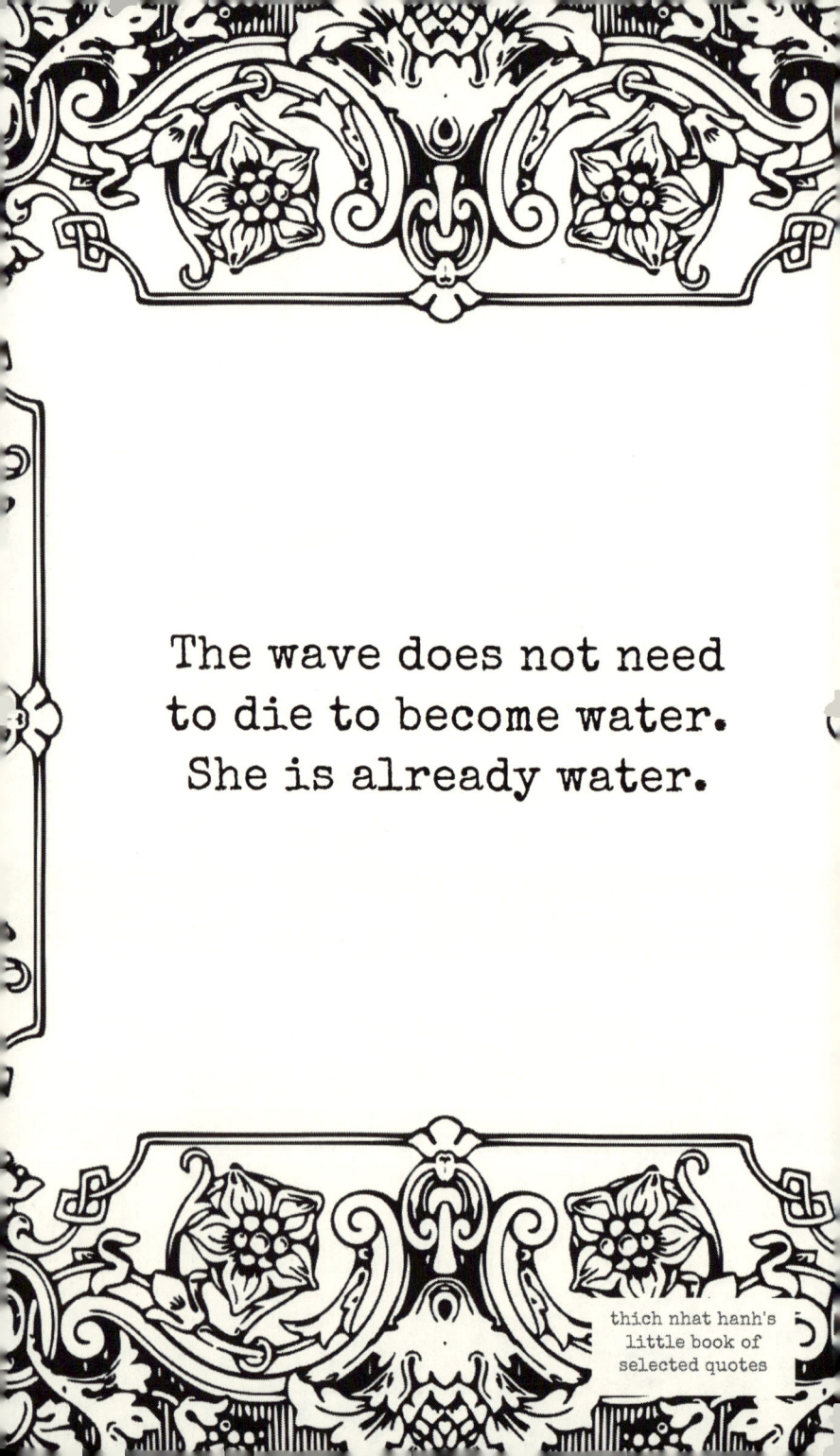

Our own lives are the instruments with which we experiment with truth.

thich nhat hanh's little book of selected quotes

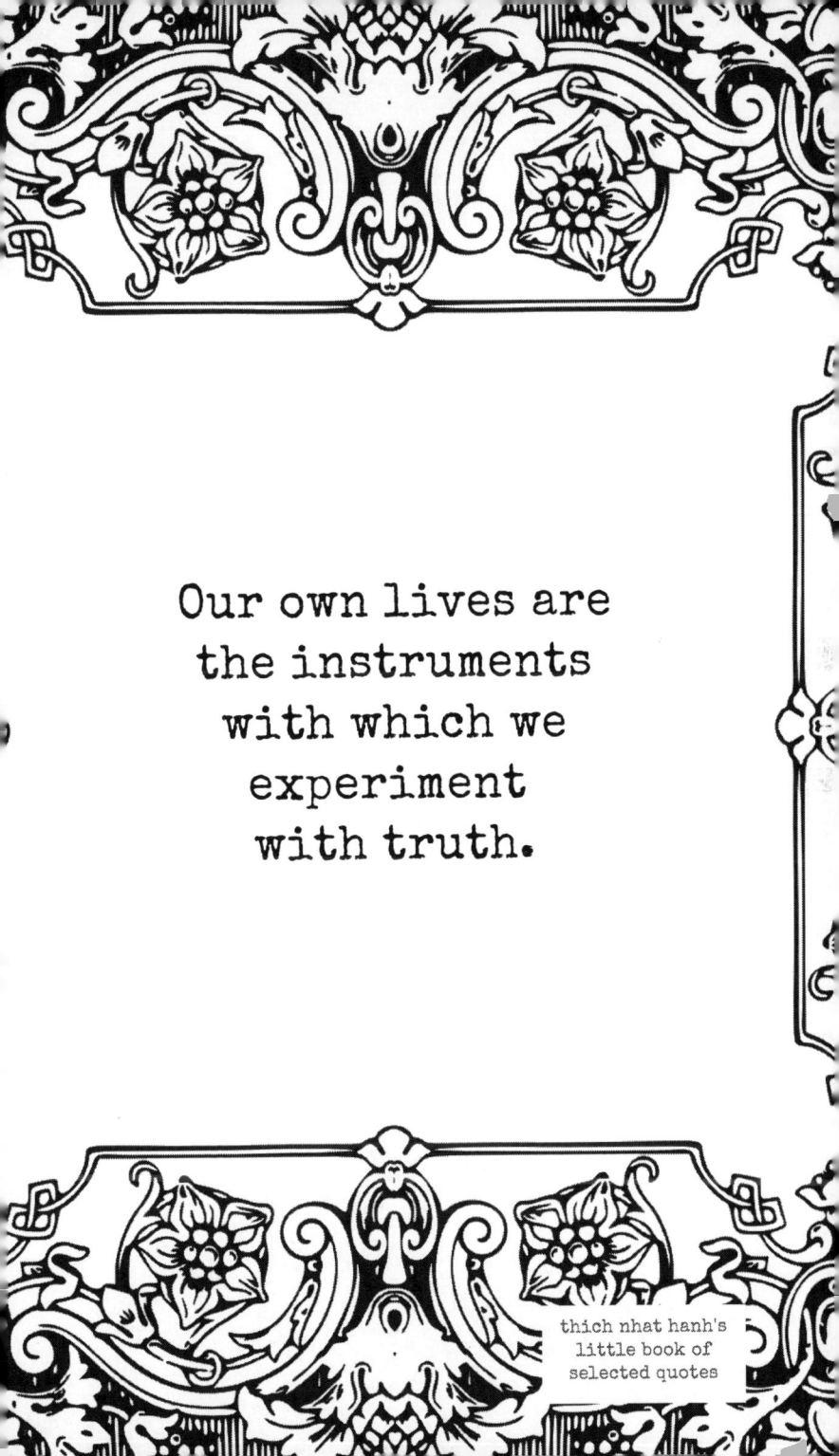

In mindfulness one is not only restful and happy, but alert and awake. Meditation is not evasion; it is a serene encounter with reality.

thich nhat hanh's little book of selected quotes

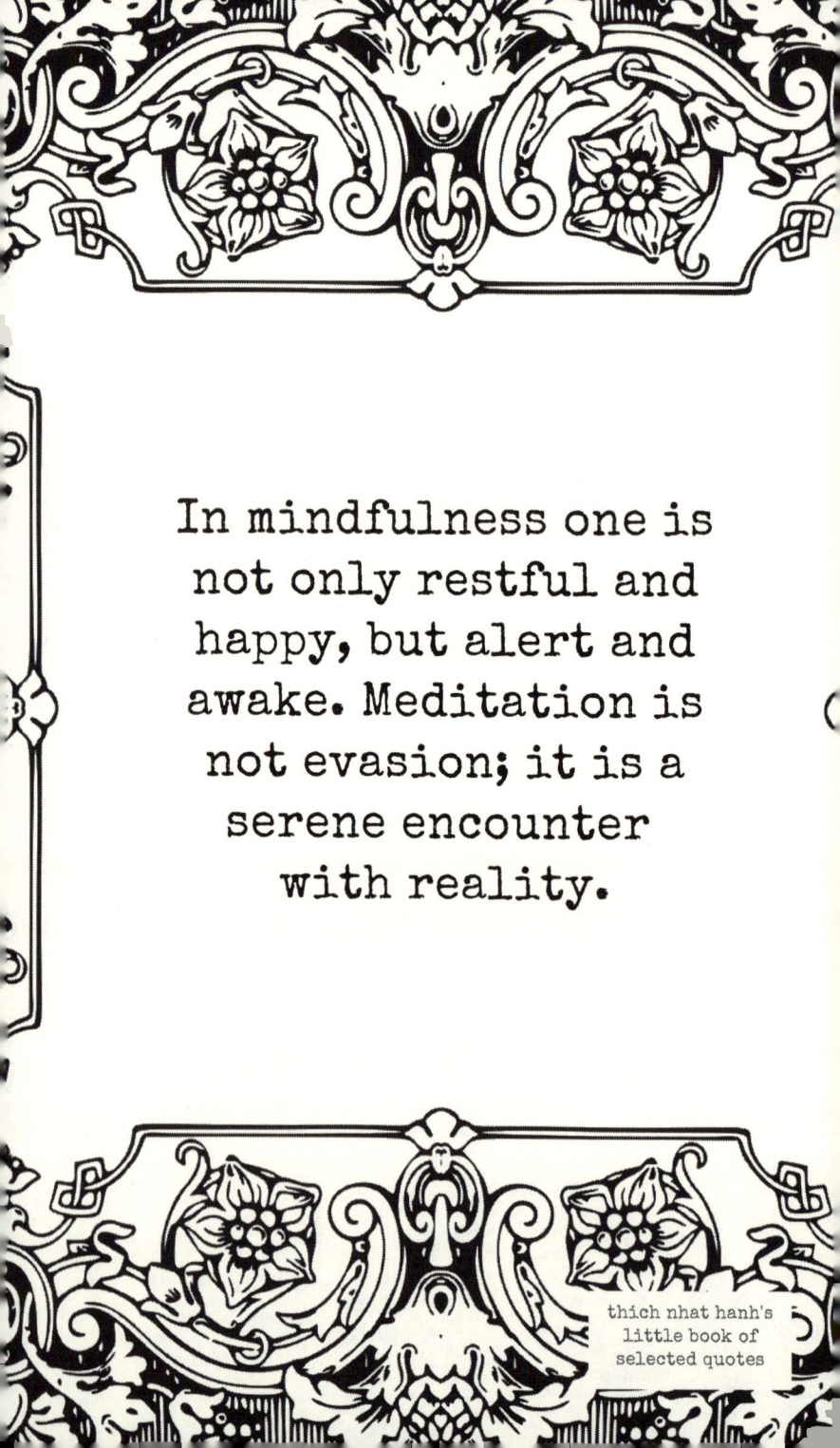

If we are not fully ourselves, truly in the present moment, we miss everything.

thich nhat hanh's little book of selected quotes

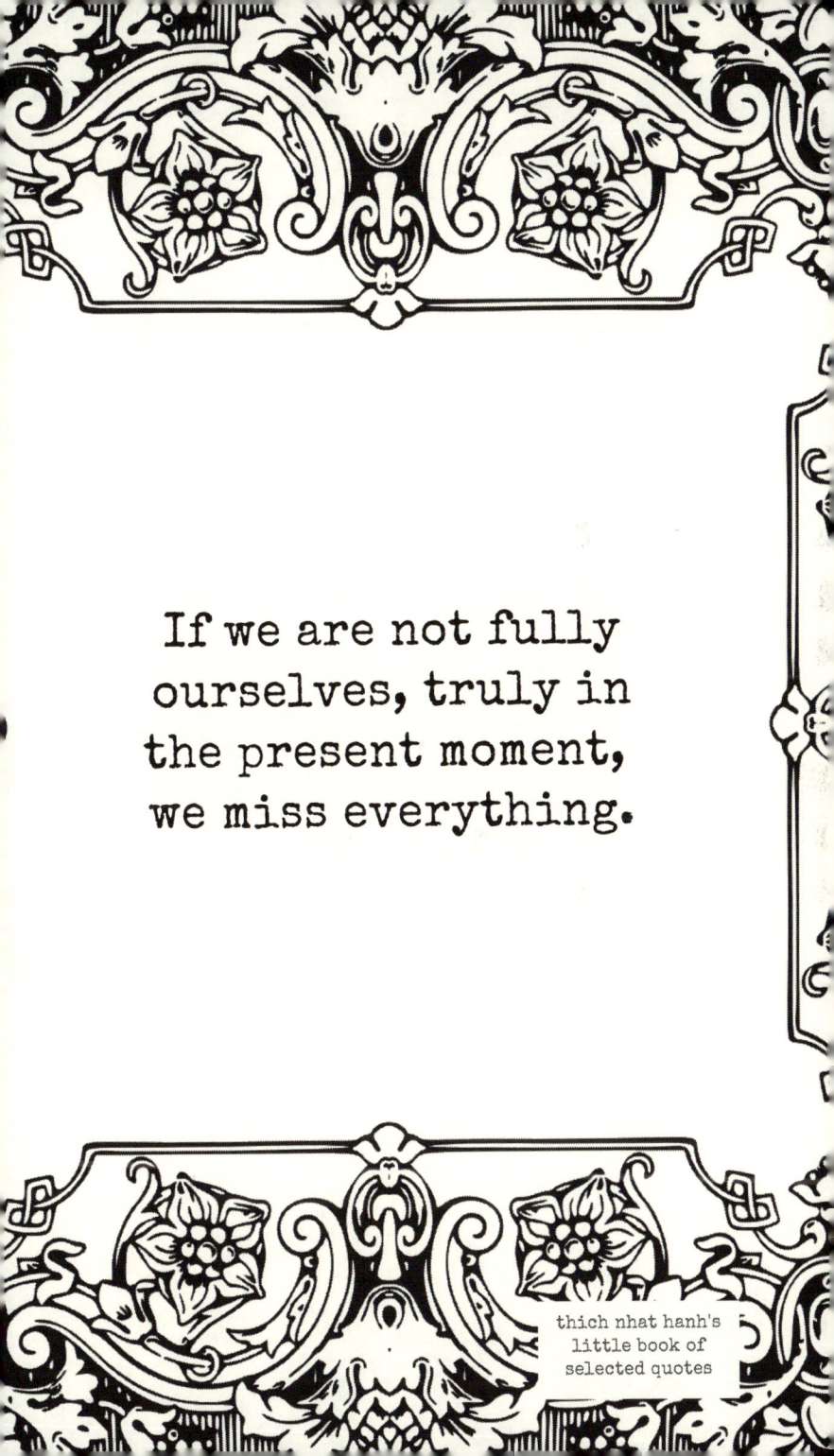

The seed of suffering in you may be strong, but don't wait until you have no more suffering before allowing yourself to be happy.

thich nhat hanh's little book of selected quotes

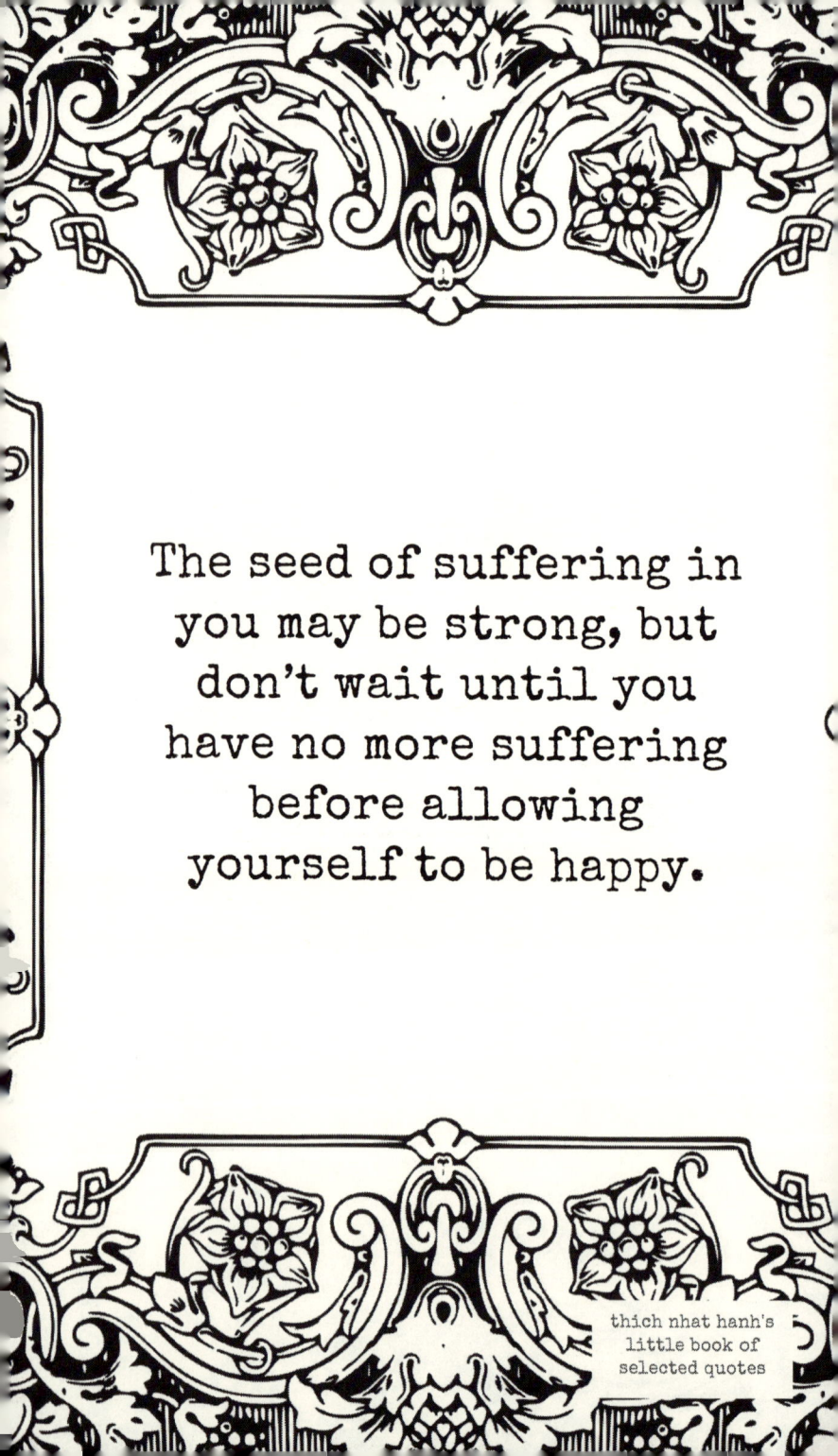

An oak tree is an oak tree. That is all it has to do. If an oak tree is less than an oak tree, then we are all in trouble.

thich nhat hanh's little book of selected quotes

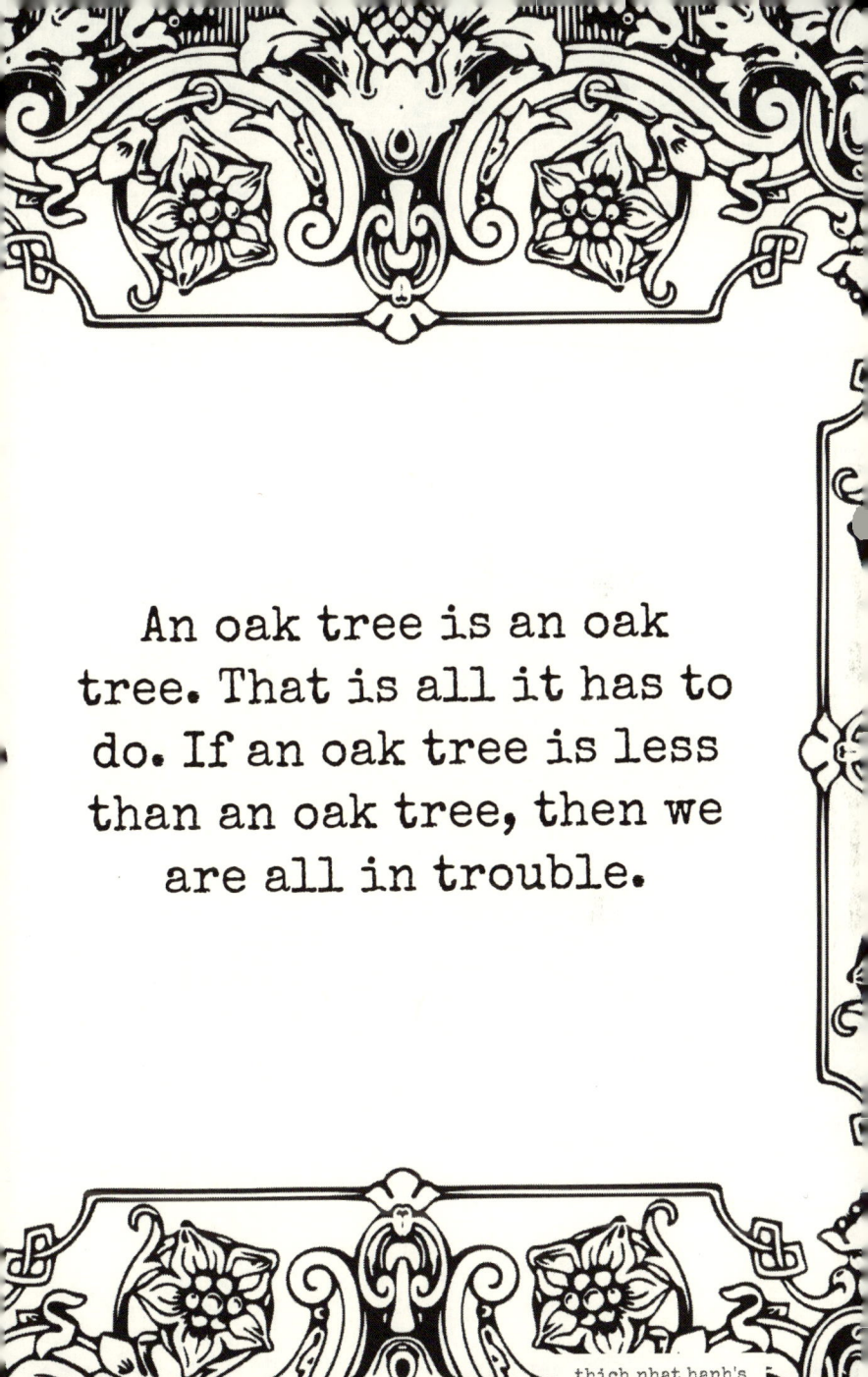

Many people think excitement is happiness.... But when you are excited you are not peaceful. True happiness is based on peace.

thich nhat hanh's little book of selected quotes

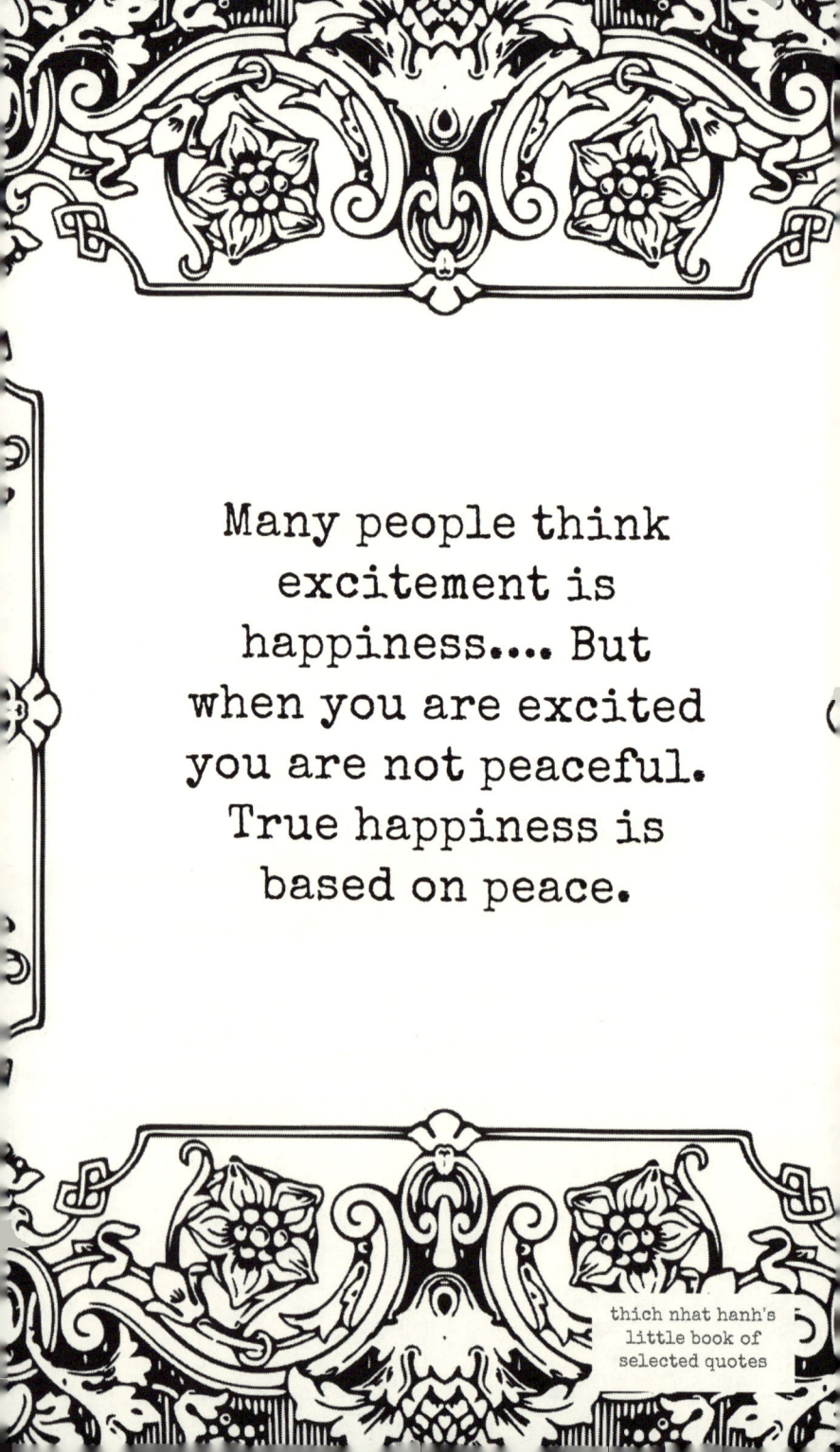

My actions are my only true belongings. I cannot escape the consequences of my actions. My actions are the ground on which I stand.

thich nhat hanh's little book of selected quotes

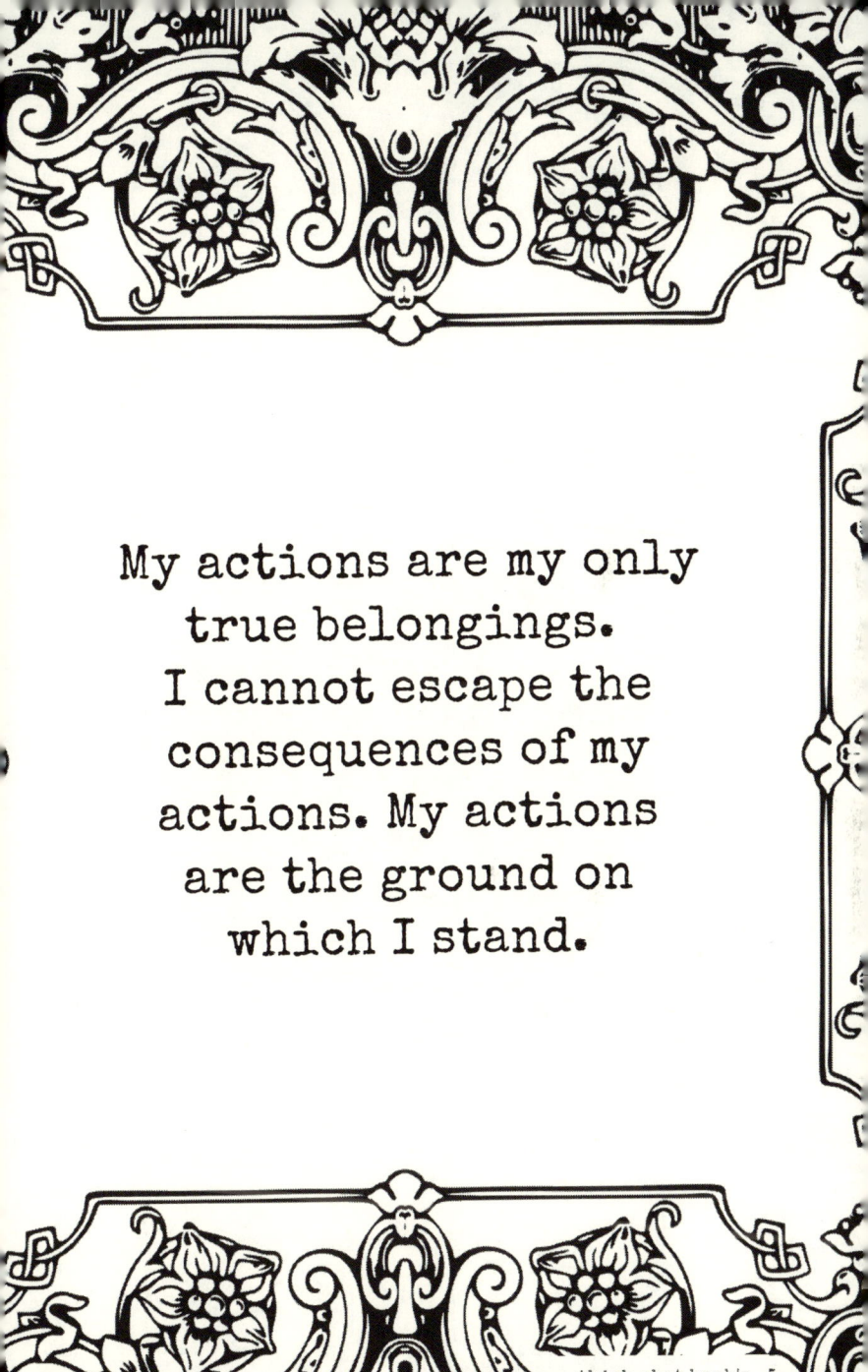

I am determined
to practice
deep listening.
I am determined
to practice
loving speech.

thich nhat hanh's
little book of
selected quotes

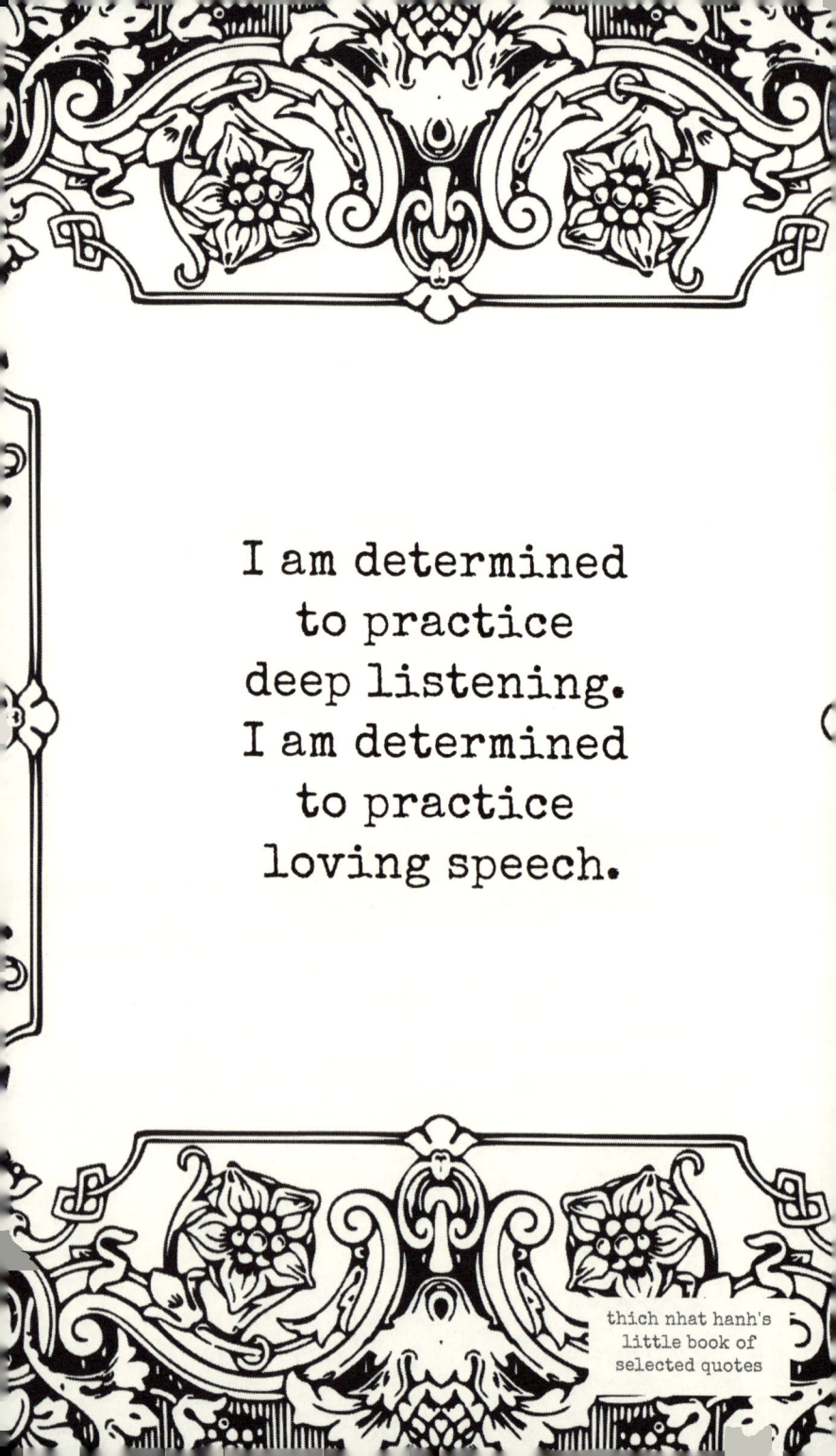

Anxiety, the illness of our time, comes primarily from our inability to dwell in the present moment.

thich nhat hanh's little book of selected quotes

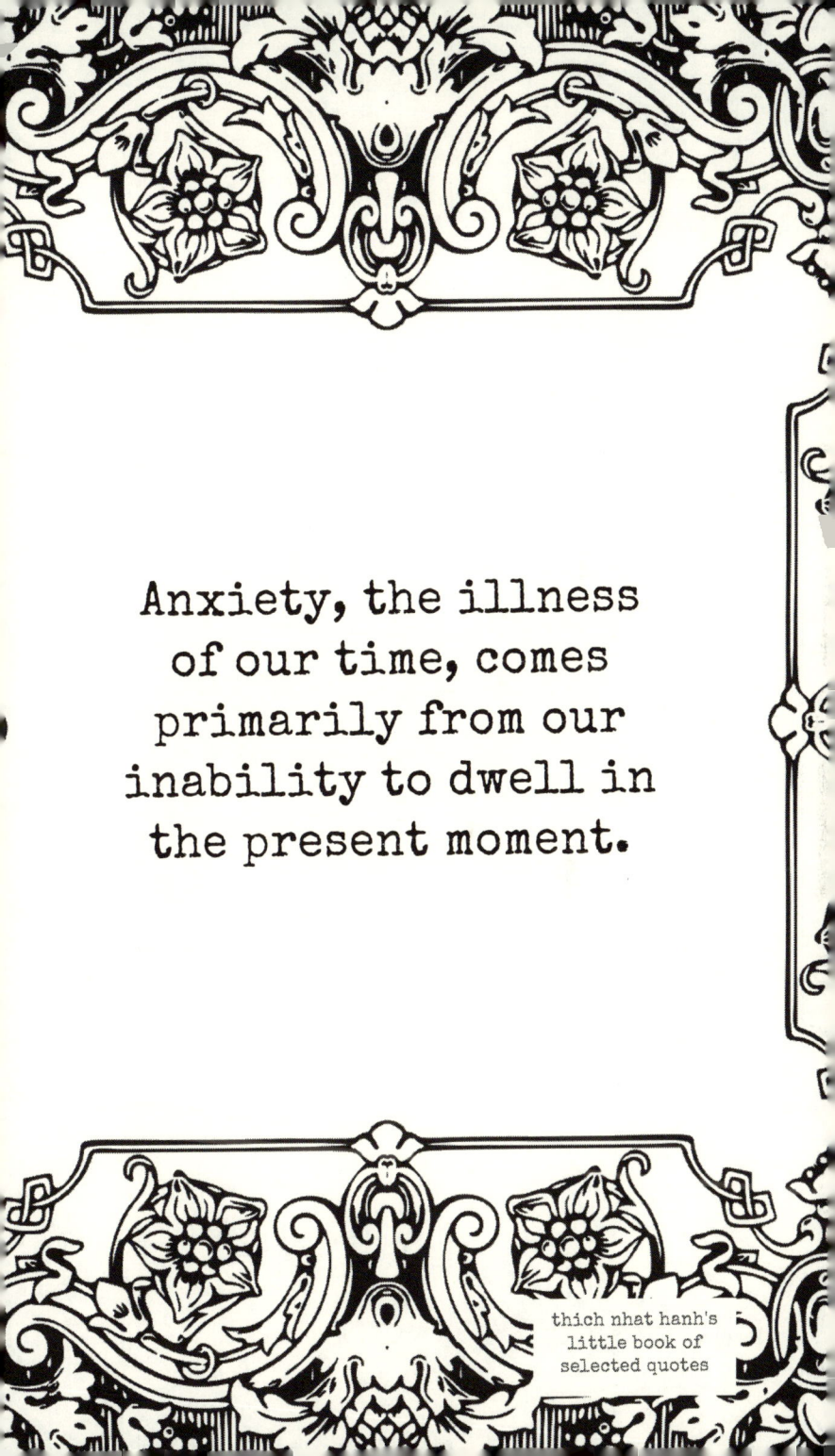

We will not just say,
I love him very much,
but instead, I will do
something so that he will
suffer less. The mind of
compassion is truly
present when it is
effective in removing
another person's
suffering.

thich nhat hanh's
little book of
selected quotes

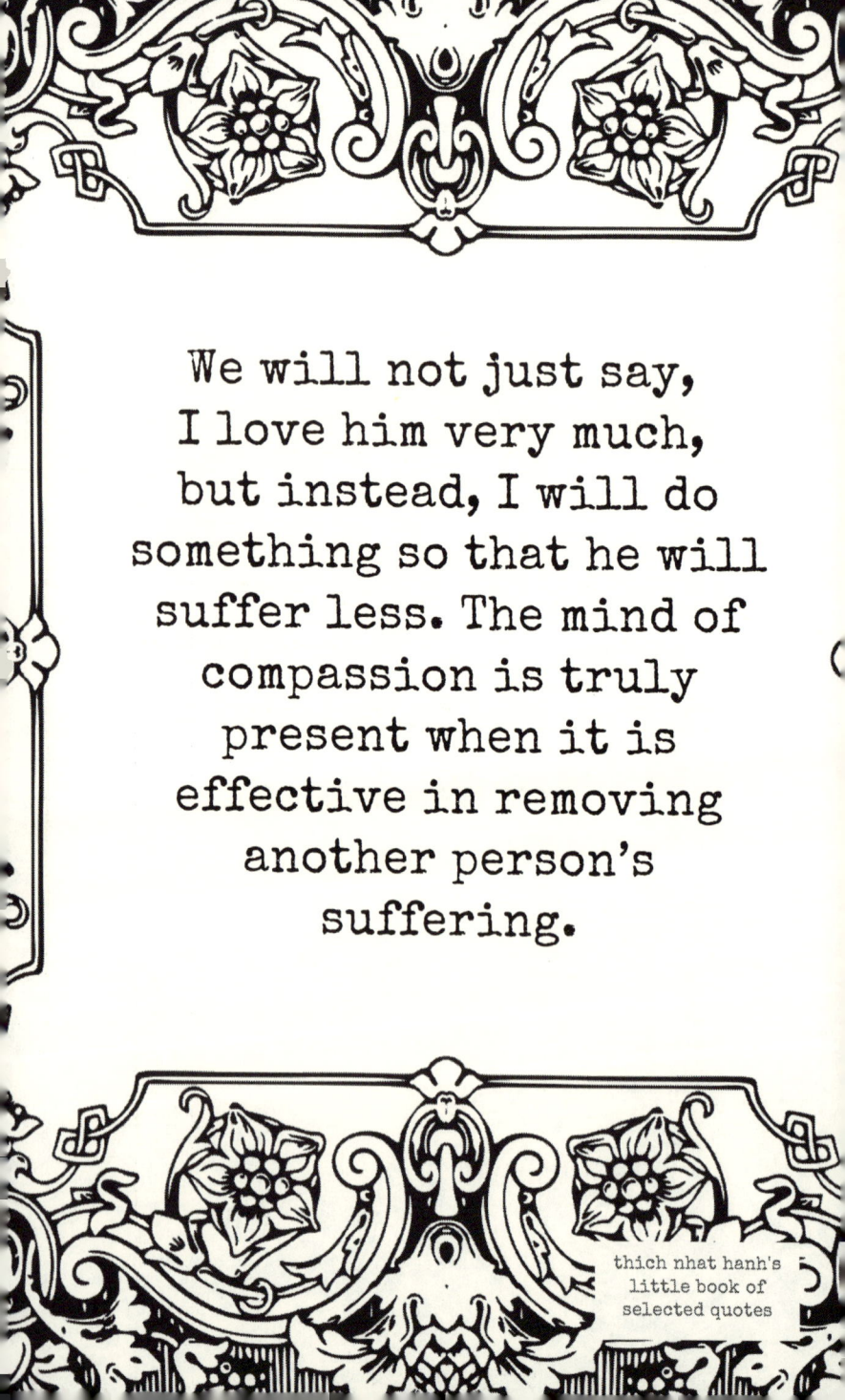

Attachment to views is the greatest impediment to the spiritual path.

thich nhat hanh's little book of selected quotes

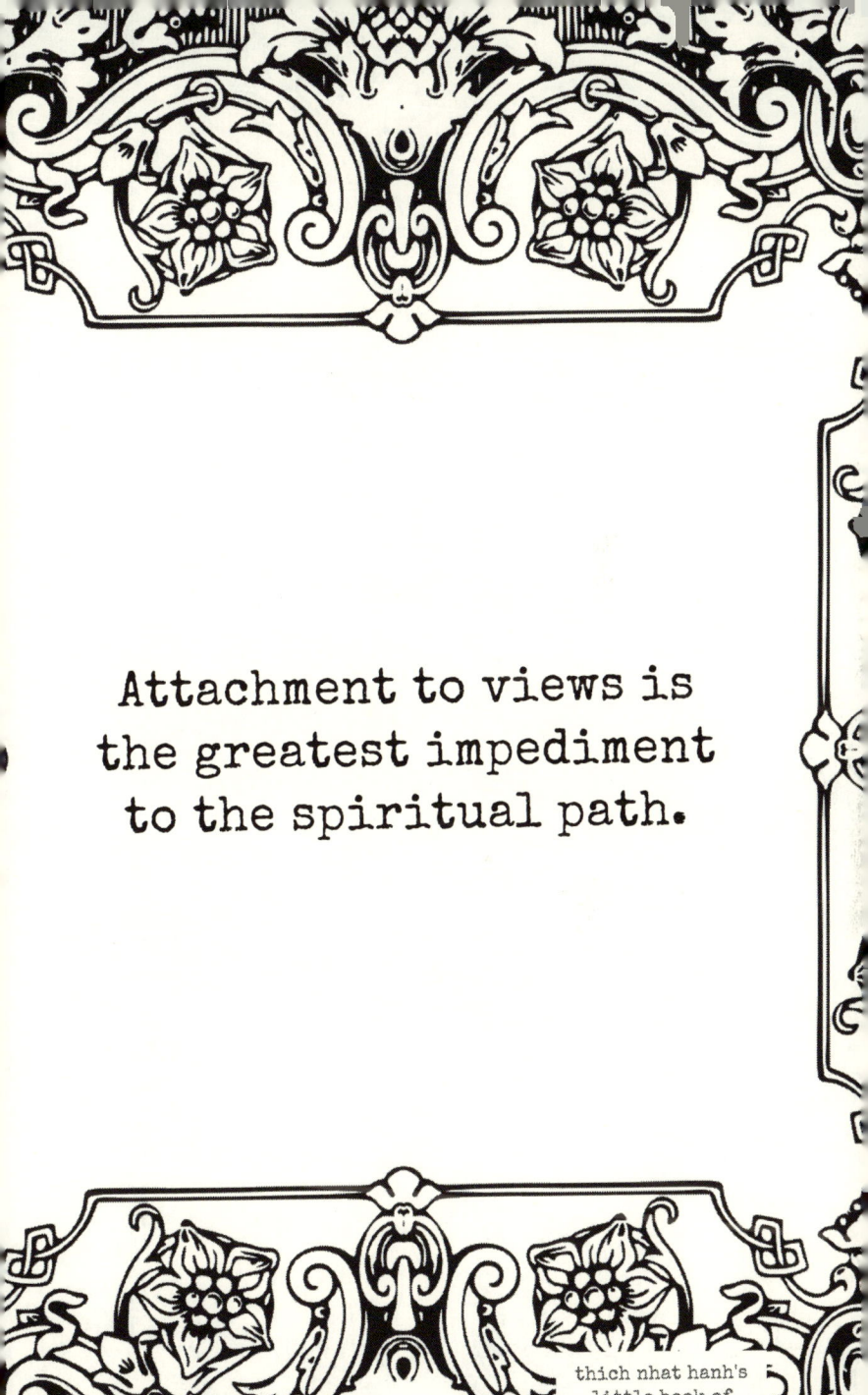

Our own life has to be our message.

thich nhat hanh's
little book of
selected quotes

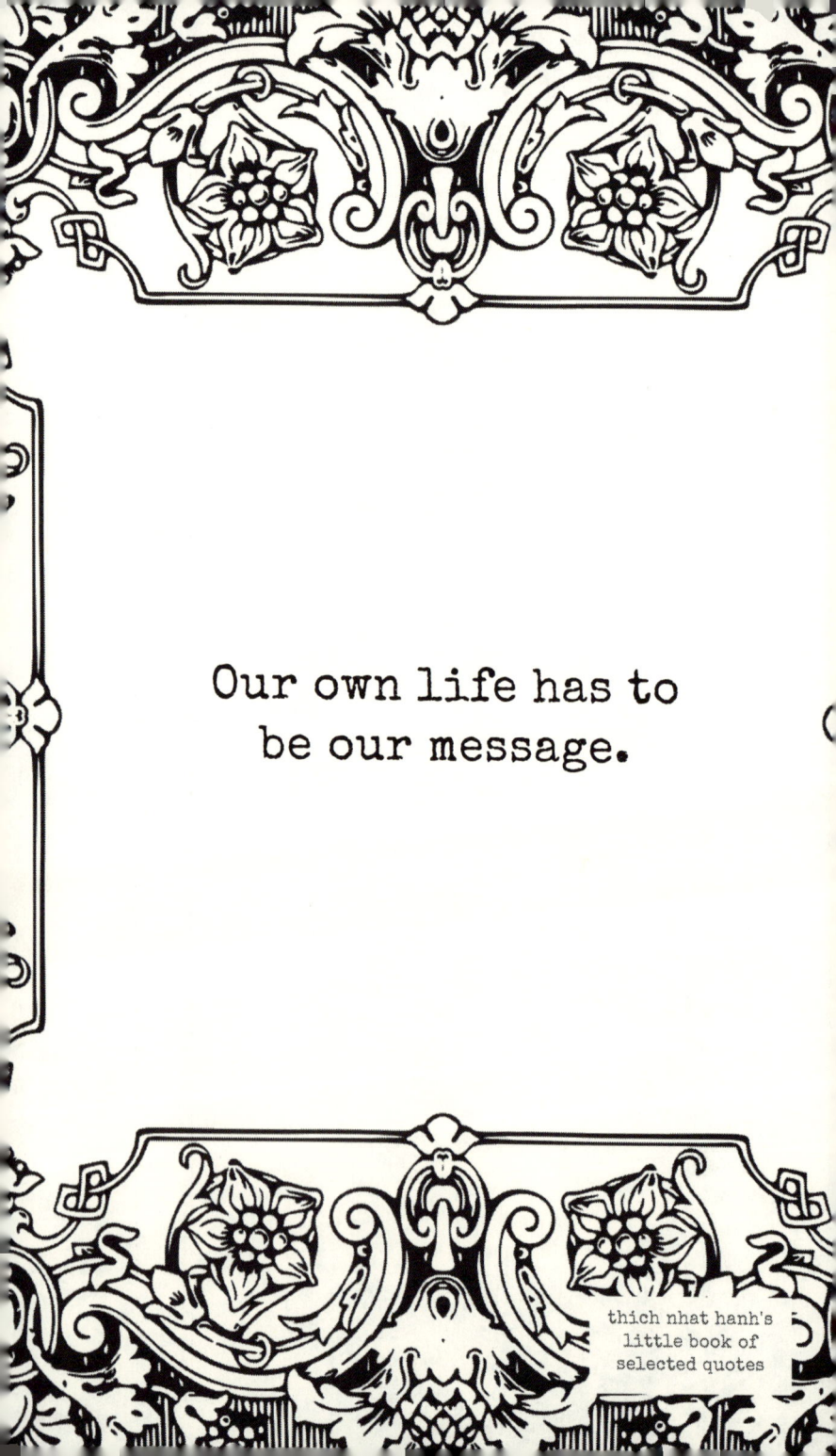